S0-BZE-822

A PRIMER FOR PSYCHOTHERAPISTS

By

KENNETH MARK COLBY, M.D.

ADJUNCT IN PSYCHIATRY, MOUNT ZION HOSPITAL, SAN FRANCISCO; CLINICAL ASSOCIATE, SAN FRANCISCO INSTITUTE OF PSYCHOANALYSIS; FORMERLY LECTURER IN PSYCHIATRY, DEPARTMENT OF SOCIAL WELFARE, UNIVERSITY OF CALIFORNIA

A RONALD PRESS PUBLICATION

JOHN WILEY & SONS

New York • Chichester • Brisbane • Toronto

Copyright, 1951, by
JOHN WILEY & SONS

All Rights Reserved

Reproduction or translation of any part of this work beyond that
permitted by Sections 107 or 108 of the 1976 United States
Copyright Act without the permission of the copyright owner is
unlawful. Requests for permission or further information should be
addressed to the Permissions Department, John Wiley & Sons, Inc.

10
VR-VR

ISBN   0-471-06901-9

Library of Congress Catalog Card Number: 51-10248

PRINTED IN THE UNITED STATES OF AMERICA

10   9   8   7   6   5   4   3   2

To Yvonne

PREFACE

Like all primers, this is a small book of elementary principles written for beginners. The beginners in psychotherapy addressed here are all those with a professional intent in pursuing the subject—internes or residents in psychiatric hospitals and clinics, practicing psychiatrists, clinical psychologists, and psychiatric social workers.

One of the first needs of beginners in psychotherapy is an operational definition, i.e., a clear idea of what is done and for what purposes. During psychotherapeutic interviews a therapist and a patient carry on a verbal interchange in which the productions of the patient are interpreted to him by the therapist with the goal of relieving the patient's neurotic or psychotic distress and providing him with some understanding (and hence mastery) of his psychological motivations. As is true of all medicine, psychotherapy is not an exact science but a practical art, in which general principles of scientific derivation are followed and interpreted according to the judgment of the individual therapist as to the best course of treatment for each patient. For the beginner this is indeed a difficult situation, and there is little in the literature that is specifically intended to help him.

This book has been written in an attempt to supply this lack. Psychotherapy, like other medical specialties, is best learned in apprenticeship to an experienced practitioner. As the reflective reader will discover for himself, it is very difficult to reproduce the experiences of psychotherapy in writing or to absorb them fully from reading an objective recital of the facts. The book is offered as a companion to the indispensable personal instruction and observation which provide the practical base for psychotherapy.

Except for the last chapter, the book is directed to the treatment of neuroses. Since a part of the beginner's work involves the treatment of schizophrenic patients as well, a section has been added on the modifications of therapy necessary in the latter situation.

I wish to acknowledge with gratitude the helpful comments on the manuscript made by Dr. Siegfried Bernfeld and Dr. Norman Reider. The illustrative clinical examples are from my own files, and the views expressed, while few could be called original, are of course entirely my responsibility.

KENNETH MARK COLBY

San Francisco, California
January, 1951

CONTENTS

CONTENTS

A PRIMER FOR
PSYCHOTHERAPISTS

Chapter 1

PSYCHOTHERAPY—ITS AIM AND ITS BASIC THEORY

Aim

The goal of psychotherapy is to relieve the patient of distressing neurotic symptoms or discordant personality characteristics which interfere with his satisfactory adaptation to a world of people and events.

Sweeping as it sounds, this aim is actually a limited one, as the practicing psychotherapist well recognizes. Psychotherapy—including its most extensive form, psychoanalysis—is repair work. This view cannot be overemphasized. A psychotherapist should not expect great transformations equivalent to a psychological rebirth or a complete reorganization of the patient's personality. The results which can be achieved in this repair work are limited by the caliber of the original material (constitution plus young ego), the degree of damage (infantile traumas and adult frustrations), and what remains to be worked with (adult ego plus the reality situation). In people, as in clothes, some materials are finer to begin with and a repaired article is never as good as the new one. Since psychotherapy is confined to repair work, this limited aim may conflict with the beginning therapist's ambitions as well as with the patient's hopes. This point will be further discussed in Chapters 2 and 3.

The goal is further circumscribed by the aim of therapy to deal only with those areas of the personality producing major

3

disturbances. Aspects of the patient's character which are ego-syntonic and which he wants to keep are better left alone unless they are inextricably bound up with his neurotic symptoms. For example, an overtly homosexual man who develops a phobia and who wishes to retain his sexual orientation can be treated for the phobia without seeking the goal of changing his homosexual character structure to a heterosexual one. Likewise, a deeply religious patient who desires relief from an anxiety neurosis without loss of his religious beliefs is entitled to psychotherapy devoid of the aim of altering these convictions. It sometimes does happen during therapy that patients change their views on what aspects of their personality they wish to retain, particularly when this appears necessary in order to be rid of unpleasant symptoms. However, such changes are secondary outcomes and not the initial sought-after goal.

In speaking of the goal of psychotherapy, the term "cure" frequently intrudes. It requires definition. If by "cure" we mean relief of the patient's current neurotic difficulties, then that is certainly our goal. If by "cure" we mean a lifelong freedom from emotional conflict and psychological problems, then that cannot be our goal. Just as a person may suffer pneumonia, a fracture, and diabetes during his lifetime and require particular minimizing and separate treatment for each condition, so another person may experience at different times a depression, impotence, and a phobia, each requiring psychotherapy as the condition arises. Our aim is to treat the presenting problems, hoping that the work will strengthen the patient against further neurotic difficulties but realizing that therapy cannot guarantee a psychological prophylaxis.

Finally, it is not the goal of psychotherapy to produce an ideal or model person. Everyone in life must learn to withstand a certain amount of emotional tension. That the patient who has undergone psychotherapy is one who is placid, emotionless, lovable, good-natured, and guiltless, no matter what happens to him, is an illusion in which neither the patient nor the therapist must invest, however strongly our culture insists on worshiping such a psychological saint.

All this, to be sure, is the therapist's concept of the goal, and it may differ widely from what some patients have in mind when coming to be helped. Since in our time and culture the psychotherapist has come to represent an amalgam of oracle, sage, and healer, those ridden by anxieties, who in other times might have relied upon other resources, now sometimes turn to him for "happiness" or a spiritual code to live by. There is much suffering and unhappiness in the world which psychotherapy can do nothing about. And establishing rules of conduct is not our province. Hence patients searching for happiness in terms of formulas or right-wrong precepts are certain to be disappointed by a psychotherapy which has the goal only of relieving neurotic or psychotic distress.

Basic Theory

We assume that, before a therapist attempts any psychotherapy, he will have acquired a familiar acquaintance both with the main clinical facts about neurotic and psychotic behavior and with convenient working concepts of a dynamic-genetic-structural-economic nature to use in understanding this behavior. These data are admirably, if tortuously, collected in Otto Fenichel's *Psychoanalytic Theory of Neurosis*, a book which must be read very slowly, in small doses, patiently and repeatedly. However, a few aspects of the theory can profitably be reviewed at this point. All the psychotherapeutic recommendations to be made are well founded in this logically uniform theoretical system as well as in practical experience.

Our theory begins with Freud's concept of the mind as an apparatus which attempts to deal with entering volumes of excitation in order to preserve the equilibrium of a rest state. The term "rest" is not to be taken in an absolute or static sense, but as implying a flux of energy changes within a limited range. As stimuli disturb the rest state by increasing tension, the mind seeks to discharge or bind this tension. Mental stimuli may be external or internal. External stimuli are those features of the surrounding environment perceived by the organism. Internal stimuli are those impulses (sexual and aggressive wishes) set going by biochemical energy changes. The young and growing mind learns, in integrating its internal needs with its environment, through thousands of reward-punishment experiences, to curb, moderate, channelize, displace, and postpone its wishes.

More specifically, a wish (internal tension-producing stimulus) may be totally gratified (tension discharged), totally denied (tension bound), or both gratified and denied (partially discharged, partially bound). The binding process is thought of in terms of defenses. In topographic terms, wish-impulses from the id are regulated by the defenses of the ego and superego.

In the normal state there is a harmonious relationship between wishes and defenses so that tensions are successfully managed with a satisfactory preservation of a relative rest state. A neurosis, on the contrary, is characterized (but not defined) by a neurotic conflict. That is, the compromise achieved by a wish and a conflicting defense has not successfully discharged or bound tension. Various clinical symptoms result from this type of conflict. We speak of a neurotic conflict, but there is usually more than one in a given neurosis. Since we treat them one at a time, it becomes a matter of convenience to speak of "conflict" in the singular. For the most part the patient is unaware of the nature, extent, or significance of his conflicts. Being unconscious and hence inaccessible, neurotic conflicts exert an all the greater influence on his mental life.

In theory, the goal of psychotherapy is to produce a favorable change in the disturbed balance of a conflictual wish-defense system, thus allowing a fuller gratification of the wish or at least a more suitable compromise. Since we cannot, to any great extent, influence by psychological means the origin of biological processes per se (wish-impulses), in therapy we manage a wish-defense conflict by modifying the defense or ego component. Ideally we would like solely to attenuate or eradicate a pathogenic defense, but in actual practice, we probably annul some defenses while reinforcing others, the latter aiding binding rather than discharging functions. With the return of a relative equilibrium in a wish-defense conflict, tension diminishes and the symptoms decrease or vanish.

Next, let us consider the theory of the maneuvers by which this goal is reached. As the patient talks, the therapist listens and tries in his own mind to sort out, from the mass of thoughts, memories, and feelings the patient presents, an important neurotic conflict or group of conflicts. That is, the therapist attempts to see clearly the wish-defense system involved in a symptom-producing conflict. By various tactics (see below) he then brings this area to the attention of the patient in whom up until that time the ingredients of the conflict have been unconscious. As the defense of the conflict is brought to the patient's consciousness through verbalization, the motivation for the defense (affects of anxiety, guilt, shame, disgust regarding the wish) receives attention in terms of the patient's present and past life experience. Thereby the patient's "reasonable adult ego" is given the freedom to judge and relinquish this particular anachronistic defense as its motivation is seen to be of infantile origin.

Such is the strategy. The tactics by which the therapist influences a patient in this way now deserve comment. Statements by the therapist, i.e., interpositions and interpretations, are the chief tools used to change the defense or ego component of a neurotic conflict. These statements are made in reference to the patient's communications in two main areas, transferences and resistances, which represent the neurotic defenses in action in the therapy situation. By *transference* we mean the repetitious attempt, made unknowingly by the patient, to perceive and treat the therapist as an important figure of his childhood. *Resistances* are those defenses which operate in and against the therapeutic process to prevent an uncovering and a dissolution of the neurotic conflict. Thus, in theory, a transference is one form of resistance. Illustrations of types of interpretations, transferences, and resistances are given in Chapter 7.

By now surely an important question has arisen. Isn't all this psychoanalysis? Freud said that any therapy which handles transference and resistance is psychoanalysis. Indeed, as presented, our theory of neurosis and our concept of the dynamics of cure are psychoanalytic. But though the theory is the same, the actual practice is somewhat different. These differences between psychotherapy and psychoanalysis are determined by several factors, the more important of which are mentioned below.

Time considerations are outstanding determinants in distinguishing psychotherapy from classical psychoanalysis. Since in psychotherapy both the therapist and the patient have less time available than is necessary for psychoanalysis, the frequency of interviews and the total duration of therapy are less. The time pressure prompts the therapist to be more active in questioning and in focusing the patient's attention on a significant conflict. This in turn means that the patient's communications are less in the nature of prolonged free association than they are a combination of conversation and associations. In psychotherapy, early childhood is less thoroughly explored and dreams are not exhaustively interpreted. The cases selected for psychotherapy (cf. Chapter 2) differ in some respects from analytic cases, as may the degree to which a therapeutic goal is attainable. In psychotherapy probably more pathogenic defenses are strengthened, by support, guidance, and reassurance, than in psychoanalysis, which attempts primarily to eradicate defenses. Finally, whether the full transference neurosis, in which most or all of the patient's conflicts become centered about the therapist, theoretically can or should be avoided in psychotherapy is a much discussed question. In practice, though the transference neurosis may not develop to the degree observed in psychoanalysis, there is always a transference aspect and in some cases it may blossom with full intensity. Thus psychotherapy and psychoanalysis have a similar theory of neurosis and treatment, but they differ quantitatively and to some extent qualitatively in their theory, and hence practice, of technique.

With this sketch of the psychotherapeutic aim and its theory in mind, let us now turn to the subject and object of these concepts—the patient.

Chapter 2

THE PATIENT

Psychological Appraisal

Before he enters your office door, the patient has happily escaped being labeled with the imposing but humanly empty diagnostic terms of clinical psychiatry. He is neither a "compulsive" nor a "hysteric," but a human being like any other—a labile organism adapting to a culture. A psychologically more understanding view of him can be obtained from the consideration of three aspects which he presents: (a) his organism, (b) his ego, and (c) his environment.

Organism.—That the patient has a body and a concept of it is important to remember however psychologically or culturally minded the therapist may become. Satisfying biological needs for food, drink, warmth, shelter, etc. occupy a share of his thinking in adjusting to both physical and cultural conditions. What he thinks of his body as a source of pleasure or discomfort and how he perceives reality in terms of this body concept are integral to all of his ideas and imagery. Body size or shape, beauty or ugliness, wholeness or handicap, and skill or clumsiness also may represent significant determinants in psychological processes.

Equally important for the psychotherapist to realize is the impact various bodily illnesses have had on the patient's concept of himself. In addition, these illnesses have subjected him to interpersonal experiences in doctor-patient relationships which will have relevance to his approach to you.

Ego.—Here I use the term "ego" to mean interacting wish-defense systems (including the superego as a crystallization of special systems), organized and differentiated to mediate between external world and internal strivings. The present-day ego of a patient can be understood only through consideration of its historical development through successive stages of maturation. Learning and growth experiences of childhood result in the molding, congealing, and solidifying of the ego process which become characteristic for the patient in the management of his life. Using E. Erikson's attractive terms, in forming his unconscious life-plan, a person organizes his past experience to prepare for and meet the future.

This ego serves the patient well if it can make a reasonable judgment of the consequences of his behavior, tolerate the tensions of inevitable reality frustrations, and allow sufficient impulse-gratification. A less reliable ego will fail in one or all of these functions. An ego may be further implemented by an above-average intellect, a vigorous competitive drive, or certain talents and skills.

Environment.—By "environment" let us understand culture, i.e., the mores and values of a social group, or according to C. Kluckhohn, "a set of explicit and implicit designs for living which people who live together share." His family as a lever through which a culture exerts its force, his job, his friendships, and perhaps his religion involve activities through which the patient strives to obtain material and moral supplies, and all combine to regulate his social status and self-esteem.

I have mentioned these three personal aspects of the patient (organism, ego, cultural environment) at this time, not as a reverent bow to the traditional cliché of "the patient as a whole," but to encourage you when evaluating a patient to think frequently in these terms rather than in those of diagnostic entities. Even after you have made a clinical and dynamic diagnosis, for whatever therapeutic, prognostic, or administrative reasons, it is therapeutically important not to view the patient as a static nosological entity but as a group of dynamic forces in flux as they advance, shift, and retreat in the interpersonal relationships of a culture.

Who Comes to Therapy

When we consider that people who seek psychotherapy are stigmatized in spite of a historically recent but glacially slow change in this cultural attitude, it is amazing that so many do come. Though of all types of personality, the individuals who look for such help often have traits in common.

For example, persons from the two lowest socioeconomic groups (lower-lower and upper-lower in L. Warner's hierarchy) rarely come spontaneously and voluntarily. They are directed to see a psychiatrist by either their physicians, a casework agency, a court, or a clinic. In each of these instances the patient is forced to come by some implied threat, otherwise he would never consider consulting a psychotherapist voluntarily. A few upper-lowers with extreme magical hopes or the prospect of secondary gains are exceptions to this. Most patients who come under their own motivational steam represent the middle and upper groups.

Another common denominator is the degree of education and literacy. Those who are accustomed to dealing in words and ideas and who think *about* their thoughts and behavior comprise the bulk of patients who spontaneously apply for psychotherapy.

A third characteristic is a type of character formation. If

all or most of a person's character traits are ego-syntonic and cause him few reality difficulties, he feels no need for psychotherapy. It is when an important character trait fails in its defensive function or produces some discomforting reality frustration that the patient seeks help. Yet there are certain neurotic characters with one or both of the latter conditions who usually avoid psychotherapy. Antisocial characters ("psychopaths"), some sexual deviants (voyeurs, sexual masochists, etc.), many alcohol and drug addicts, and other impulsive personalities rarely wish sincerely to change their basic personality structure. They come to the psychotherapist only when forced, for secondary gains, or if they develop extremely unpleasant symptoms. Hence it is usually the case that most voluntary patients possess a character structure of some reliability and social conformity.

Why He Comes

Next let us consider forces which propel people toward psychotherapy, omitting such obvious motives as to obey a court order, to obtain case-work funds, to insure continuation of a pension, etc.

Some patients are referred for psychotherapy who have consulted their physicians for physical symptoms and learned that no organic basis for them could be found. Two factors play a part here: (a) the patient's readiness and willingness to accept such a maneuver and (b) the skill of the doctor in advising such a referral. Many patients with physical symptoms are unable to accept the idea of psychotherapy and its implications and either don't show up or break off after a couple of interviews. A few others are able to see their symptoms as a result of internal emotional conflicts and profit from a psychotherapeutic experience. Some doctors with a genuine feeling for people are quite gifted in suggesting psychotherapy without assaulting the patient's self-esteem and without making him feel that he is being sloughed off as a nuisance. There are others, however, who make a mess of things by curtly dismissing the patient as a "neurotic who ought to be psychoanalyzed" or by promising the patient a quick cure if he will just stop bothering him and see a psychiatrist a few times.

Other people who may influence the patient to come include friends and relatives. It is futile to attempt psychotherapy with someone who comes only to appease a goading relative or loved one. These patients lump you with their dominators, and the resultant transference resistances augur a poor prognosis for therapy.

Among more intrapersonal and conscious forces are those represented in the motives of the intellectually curious (writers, artists), searchers for keys (cultists, mystics), and the current normality worshipers. For these persons the therapist may be only a teacher of lore, and, though the therapy may add some halo of prestige to the patient in the eyes of his comrades, it usually does little to change his neurosis.

Finally, the patient may feel an urge to apply for psychotherapy when he suffers various unpleasant symptoms while realizing that they are in some way connected with his own emotional-psychological make-up and that with help the latter can be changed. He is, of course, a suitable patient, in contrast to the former examples.

This leads us to discuss further the various criteria which help in the selection of cases for psychotherapy.

Who is Chosen

Psychotherapy is not for everyone. This undemocratic fact may conflict with your belief as a physician that all who ask for help should receive it. However, it is an unshirkable reality that there are many people with neuroses who do not respond to the psychotherapeutic process (at least the one described in this book) favorably and proportionately enough to make the time and effort put in by both parties worth while. Hence one should have some ideas about which patients to send away and which to attempt to treat.

Freud felt that a suitable person for psychotherapy was one with a "reasonable degree of education and a fairly reliable character." Perhaps we can elaborate on and add to these qualifications through a description of two abstractions—the most suitable and the least suitable patient. Neither one of these persons exists, but as abstractions they will serve to clarify our topic.

Most Suitable Type.—He, or she, is someone between sixteen and fifty years of age and of average or above-average intelligence. (I omit any consideration of child therapy in this volume). His intellect allows him to be articulate and imaginative in expressing himself and to be able to grasp another's almost purely verbal communications. He has shown some achievement in a competitive job or a social group. He is not criminal, and his neurosis does not completely handicap him. A reasonable part of his ego permits him to step back and observe himself with some objectivity. He can see fate as mostly character and not as the "rough tyranny of circumstance." He shows courage in facing and in revealing unflattering aspects of himself. His reality situation is not overwhelming, and the secondary gains his neurosis gleans from it are small. He readily grasps the idea of participating with the therapist to form a team engaged in a joint effort. Finally, he wishes (consciously, anyway) to change his attitudes or ways of life in order to help himself, and he makes sincere attempts to do so.

Least Suitable Type.—He, or she, is of low or below-average intelligence and is generally unthinking in relation to himself. Either his complaints are all physical or else he views them as the result of some organic disease. His environment provides maximal secondary gains for a hardy neurosis. Magical thinking plays a large part in his thought processes, and his reality sense is severely impaired. A speech or hearing handicap and a language or culture barrier may further complicate matters. A storm of acute affects may make him unreachable through words, or, though he is calm, he may not "get" the therapist's questions and the simplest interpretations may soar over his head. His character is infantile, and his impulses are voiceless. He might be thought of by anyone as an unreliable person.

These overdrawn abstractions designate opposite ends of a broad scale with many intermediate variations. In choosing a patient for psychotherapy with the hope of a successful outcome, it is understandably wiser to select the person who stands closer in the scale to the most suitable. The actual technique of selection and rejection of patients is discussed in Chapter 6.

What He Fears

Every patient has certain conscious and unconscious fears and hopes regarding psychotherapy before as well as during the process. This and the following section will deal briefly with some of them.

Among the fears concerning therapy which may loom in the patient's consciousness is that of being found crazy. Or he may dread that he will be told that he is basically a homosexual or some other (to him) loathsome type of deviant. He may worry that your interpretations will one day constitute a surprise ambush, suddenly uncovering some very disturbing aspect of himself. Many patients are frightened that they will become too dependent on the therapist, thus giving him too great a power over their lives. Some fear his contempt, and others fear his love.

Unconsciously the patient's chief fear is that of changing his neurotic structures, since they are at least familiar, if unsuccessful, solutions and they provide some gratifications. Each patient also has his own particular unconscious fear of psychotherapy depending on the various meanings it may have for him.

What He Hopes

Again using the division between "conscious" and "unconscious," every patient naturally has the conscious hope of being helped. In the process he may expect that he will be guided and advised, taught and encouraged. Also he hopes a change will *happen* to him spontaneously, without willful effort on his part.

Unconsciously the patient has a magical belief in the therapist's parental omnipotent ability "to make it better." He hopes to impress you favorably and thereby gain your love and admiration, perhaps even permanently, as in a friendship or marriage. Though it is a contradiction, side by side with this desire may be the wish to make your office an arena and therapy a duel. Also there are patients with an unconscious wish for punishment who hope that the therapy will *not* succeed, thus proving that they are really hopeless. To the apprentice this concept often seems to be merely a comforting rationalization for therapeutic failure, but at one time or another he will be in a position to observe just such a mechanism in action.

Thus far we have considered the patient actually before he has become a participant in psychotherapy. Since therapy is a process involving two people, we should now examine in some detail the other person before we describe what goes on between them.

Chapter 3

THE THERAPIST

If we were to describe the requirements and qualifications of a good psychotherapist, they could perhaps be listed as follows. He should have:

1. A body of knowledge concerning normal and pathological thought and behavior in our culture.
2. A logically cohesive group of theoretical concepts which are convenient in understanding this thought and behavior.
3. Technical experience in therapeutically integrating observations with concepts through clinical work with patients.
4. Intuition as a practiced and controlled ability to read between the lines and empathically grasp what the patient means and feels beyond the face value of what he says.
5. Awareness of his own inner wishes, anxieties, and defenses and their influence on his therapeutic techniques.

Knowledge, theory, experience, and intuition are matters of learning plus talent. Self-awareness is gained only through frequent and honest consideration of our own psychological operations.

The patient never forgets, nor should we, that he is talking to another *person* and what he thinks about this person determines to a large extent what he says. Some of his opinions are transferences, while others may be justified by what the therapist is in reality. Obviously the therapist should be in a position to judge which is which. Hence we

will pay some attention to the therapist as an integral deter-
minant in the climate of therapy.

His Past

We might begin, as with the patient, by discussing the
therapist from the three perspectives of organism, ego, and
cultural environment. But since he can be evaluated in these
respects like any patient, we cannot add much to what has already been said in the preceding chapter.

Yet there is one decisively formative experience in the
therapist's past which warrants mention in that it has great
bearing on his fitness as a psychotherapist. This is his medical training, with both its good and its bad consequences.
The good ones are celebrated often enough without honor-
ing them here. The bad ones can bring complications into
the therapist's career, and he should be aware of these possibilities.

Outstanding among educationally induced handicaps are
the detachment and dehumanization achieved in medical
school. One learns to become interested almost entirely in
diseases per se rather than in the people who *have* the diseases. A once-active imagination may become stunted in
the name of a false scientific objectivity. The traditional
medical single cause-and-effect concept of disease narrows
the observation and sympathetic understanding of inter-
human processes. For example, a patient in the terminal
stages of a carcinoma of the pancreas, shown briefly to two
groups of students, was described by senior medical students
in terms of icteric index and metastasis, while senior college
students readily grasped the heart of the matter—the man
was dying. In matters of treatment also, medical education
directs the axis of the student's interest toward mechanisms
that can be seen and touched. It is only through repeated

therapeutic experiences with patients that his educationally ingrained distrust of treatment through verbalized ideas becomes surmounted.

Undoing these tubular views becomes one of the problems in the metamorphosis of the beginning psychotherapist. Some, though for reasons other than exposure to medical school, never seem to achieve such a rehumanization. Fortunately most therapists can overcome this limitation in much less time than it took to acquire it.

His Present

A psychotherapist is first a human being and only secondly a technician. He has become a psychotherapist as a result of the interactions of his life experiences and his own wish-defense systems. In therapeutic work, sexual and aggressive wishes mesh with ego and superego defenses in such a way as to bring emotional satisfaction and to earn a living for the therapist, now or in the future.

Each therapist has his own particular character structure, and it is of course impossible to generalize about the unique aspects which these structures present. Still there are some general emotional problems which therapists share in common as potential interferences in careful therapeutic work.

Fenichel has said that the patient's wish to be cured by a magician may be equaled by the therapist's wish to be a magician. A diplomaed authority may be unaware that he is magically convincing himself of his own omnipotence. Too, there is in every healing profession the temptation to play God, and an all-wise, all-powerful-acting therapist may soon run into unpleasant difficulties, just as new-found powers proved heady for the sorcerer's apprentice. A psychotherapist is really not God, nor even a close relative of his.

Every therapist naturally wants to cure his patients. But this wish may obscure the reality possibilities of cure or the length of time a cure will require. Overambitious therapeutic eagerness is something the beginner contends with until experience tempers his wishful concept of the quick and complete mutability of neurotic processes. When frustrated, the urge to get results may lead to countertransference difficulties.

Most beginners are aware of the sexual feelings which may arise in psychotherapy. Some recognize their hostile and aggressive attitudes toward the patient. More difficult to realize are the narcissistic needs and defenses which the therapist has at stake in the therapeutic process. When one has spent years of hard work at training to become an expert and has achieved a rather special status in our society, it may not be easy both to hold a favorable opinion of one's self and to be reminded of weaknesses, mistakes, and failures. Patients quickly learn whether or not they can produce a response when they openly doubt your knowledge, experience, or ability to help them. Those youthful in appearance have the additional problem that this characteristic may be seized on by the patient as a visible target for bombarding the therapist's self-esteem. The danger is a defense of overcompensation wherein the therapist tries too hard to demonstrate his ability, usually through overinterpretation.

The therapist may struggle with the temptation to impress the patient, perhaps by showing him how knowledgeable he is or even by attempting to maintain a papal infallibility. However, one cannot long remain infallible, since there are plenty of mistakes to be made in psychotherapy and everybody (not only beginners) makes them. Your work will never be flawless. The important thing is not that we have some degree of narcissism or that we want to be perfect, but that we are aware of when it is a narcissistic blow that is determining our reaction to the patient and when we have made a technical error.

Problems of earning a living, of his position in the community, and of his own love relationships have bearing on the therapist's professional activities. He must have some realization of how these personal factors influence his attitudes toward patients and of the fact that his own values in these areas may unduly impress him as the values others "should" have.

His Task

The therapist's task is to help the patient understand himself by bringing unconscious ideas and memories into his consciousness through the verbalization of them. It is not the job of the psychotherapist to give love, to offer himself as an example of a normal or model person, or to instruct the patient on how to live a proper life. The patient has had people for many years telling him what he should do and exactly how he should do it. For him to talk to someone who does not nag and moralize is a special experience which can permit him to grow to feel that he is a responsible adult rather than a naughty child.

In carrying out his task, the therapist's general interview attitudes are of great importance. A consistent bearing of calm, friendly, but firm gentleness proves more useful than an iron sternness, a forced joviality, or cyclic variations between the two. Although a warm, patient, and quiet good-naturedness involves risks of coddling or condescension, in the long run of work it provides the smoothest course. Kindliness does not need to mean that one avoids confronting the patient with conflicts unpleasant to him. In his recommendations for those who treat the mind, Plato wisely included knowledge, benevolence, and boldness.

Maintaining the above-described attitude for some therapists may come close to forcing one's self to play a role, and if so it carries certain disadvantages. It is unsound to try to impersonate a psychotherapist. If the way you act as a therapist is greatly different from the way you are as a person, then the façade will drain energies needed for other aspects of therapy and your patients will soon learn of this artificiality. In this connection the therapist should not attempt to "manipulate the transference," for example, acting like a father with one patient or like a brother with another. The patient must be left as freely as possible to develop spontaneously those reactions determined by his childhood experiences.

To remain serene in the face of transference aggressions and to treat patients with a gentle benevolence requires that the therapist himself be in good physical and emotional condition. If you have a pain or feel sleepy or "hung over," then you should not see patients until your malaise has cleared. Likewise, if some personal emotional problem is making a therapist uncontrollably "crabby," anxious, or depressed, then he is in no shape to do his best for the patient. Like an athlete, the psychotherapist has to keep himself in an efficient working state.

Some therapists advocate that we discuss our own feelings with the patient in an effort to demonstrate how he affects people. I cannot recommend this for beginners, who have enough trouble evaluating whether their feelings are realistic or are countertransferences. Naturally a therapist *thinks* about himself and his reactions to the patient, but this does not mean that he must *tell* the patient about his emotions. The less the patient really knows about you the greater chance he has to make transferences, which are precious material for the therapeutic process. Other devices can be more advantageous to show the patient how he operates in interpersonal relationships.

The beginner may doubt that he can be a good psychotherapist, since the whole business at first looks hopelessly complex, requiring the intellect of a genius, the talents of a master, and the emotions of a paragon. Actually it requires only average human qualities and a slightly above-average interest in using one's intellect and intuition to help others. Study and growing experience soon increase the beginner's confidence and put him more at ease in his everyday work.

Countertransferences

It is useful to divide the therapist's emotional reactions into those justified by realities in the therapeutic situation and those determined by his own inner conflicts. For example, it is natural to feel annoyed when a patient repeatedly mistreats one's furniture. But when a therapist feels outraged if a cigarette is dropped on the floor, his disproportionate response signals a countertransference problem.

When used loosely, the term "countertransference" refers to all the therapist's feelings and reactions regarding the patient. But in its limited and more accurate sense it concerns those moments when one unconsciously reacts to the patient as if he were some important figure in one's own psychological past. Of course the therapist's reaction does not literally "counter" the patient's transference. Hence the designation "collateral" or "reverse" transference perhaps conveys more of the intended meaning.

Being aware of his own feelings during an interview gives the therapist a chance to evaluate and check their expression. Countertransferences become unwanted complications when the therapist cannot control his unrealistic feelings, and in most such cases he cannot control them because he does not even realize their presence and effect.

The multiple variety of countertransference reactions might be grouped by a therapist from the standpoint of two questions which he can put to himself: (a) Who am I to myself in relationships with patients—a father, a mother, a curious child, a sibling? (b) Who are my patients to me— children, rivals, love-objects, myself? Sexual and aggressive impulses and their particular defenses interplay in all these instances. Therapists with sexual conflicts may unwittingly influence the patient to talk only of sexual matters. Therapists with anxieties concerning aggression may avoid dealing with similar material from the patient or counterphobically prod the patient into behaving aggressively toward them.

Unknowingly treating the patient as a projected part of one's self is perhaps the most common countertransference problem in beginners. Through a defense of externalization the patient may come to be unconsciously regarded by the therapist as his "bad self" who needs reforming.

A final factor to be considered by a therapist in examining his own emotions is the ability of some patients to make him feel as they wish him to feel. For example, the anxious patient who attempts to infect you with anxiety until you likewise become frightened. Or the depressed patient who describes his hopeless plight in such a way that you begin to feel just as overwhelmed and defeated as he does. Indifference and boredom felt by the therapist may be produced by a patient whose characteristic defensive maneuver is to put psychological distance between himself and the therapist and lull opposition. Such emotions experienced by the therapist are not countertransferences in the strict sense but reactions produced by the patient in the therapeutic relationship to satisfy some definite interpersonal need.

All the mechanisms thus far discussed are extremely important for the therapist to know about and to consider seriously in relation to himself. Perhaps here it would be convenient to mention the dusty controversy over whether every therapist should be psychoanalyzed. Any psychotherapist can profit from an analysis or long-term psychotherapy, and ideally every therapist should be analyzed. But for all sorts of reasons, many will not in reality have this experience. Certainly if the beginner has frank neurotic symptoms, a perversion, or some other severe character problem, he should make every effort to be analyzed. Those who do not obtain therapy for themselves can only make frequent and sincere attempts to think at length about their own psychodynamics in an effort to understand them better than those of their patients.

Chapter 4

TIME AND SPACE CONDITIONS FOR
THE INTERVIEW

The work of the therapeutic interview takes place under certain time-space conditions. To belabor such a peripheral though obvious fact may appear trivial. Yet these considerations, self-evident to the experienced therapist, present a batch of unwelcome problems to the beginner.

Time Considerations

Most patients, being eager to come, arrive for their interviews early or on time. Some are consistently a few minutes late—a phenomenon of interest to the therapist but one which can usually be ignored in the interview discussions. If a patient frequently fails to show up or comes so late as to make the brief interview of little therapeutic worth, one then knows that a major resistance is operating which must be openly dealt with by the therapist without waiting for the patient to bring it up. The following clinical examples are illustrative:

For the two previous interviews a woman had been thirty-five minutes late, leaving only fifteen minutes for therapy. On the day of this interview she was again thirty minutes late, stating that she had neglected to keep track of the time.

THER. (friendly): You've been late the last few times. What do you think this might mean?

Pt.: Last time I just forgot, and the other time I had bus trouble.

Ther.: Well, we would have to consider the possibility that coming late is an expression of your feelings about the treatment. Maybe you have doubts or reservations about coming.

Pt.: You mean that maybe I don't want to come?

Ther. (*in a manner of being open to suggestions*): Could be. Or maybe other things. What do you think?

By making the appointment-breaking or tardiness a subject of discussion, the therapist opens the area of the patient's attitudes toward therapy itself and begins to handle the resistances more directly. In passing it should be added that if a therapist fails appointments or is unpunctual, the patient may justifiably accuse him of having counter or collateral resistances.

At the other end of the interview you may find the patient trying to shorten or lengthen his session.

Pt. (*obviously feeling increased tension*): Well, I guess that's enough for today, don't you think, doctor?

Ther. (*gentle but firm*): No, our appointments run about forty-five minutes, and we still have time left. But you seem anxious to leave. Is there something on your mind that makes you uneasy?

However, with some patients (cf. page 146) it may be more expedient to allow them this defense of avoidance for some time rather than subject them to a temporary increase in anxiety.

Patients may attempt to prolong the interview by asking questions at the end requiring a lengthy discussion or trying to engage the therapist in a social conversation after he has stated that the time is up. To questions at this time one answers, "Let's discuss that next time" or "Let's talk about it some more next time before you try to make up your mind." Attempts to launch a social conversation, which may represent the isolation of therapy from real life or a striving for gratification in the transference, are parried by the therapist by not "playing the game" (Fenichel). You may simply remain silent or say, "See you next week," or, better yet, if you can, connect the material in the patient's social conversation with what was discussed during the hour.

A YOUNG woman spent the hour telling of her admiration for her father's taste. He used only the best in clothes, autos, whisky, etc. She scorned men who did not share these values. They were "slobs" with no appreciation of the finer things. At the end of the interview, while walking toward the door, she remarked, "Those are nice shoes you have. Where did you get them?" The therapist answered with a smile, "You are wondering if I come up to your father's standard or whether I'm a slob, too."

The length of the interview varies, but it should be at least forty-five or fifty minutes. Patients receiving mainly counseling or supportive guidance require less. The therapist designates termination of the interview by "Our time is up for now" or "We must end now" or "Let's stop there for today," accompanied by getting up from his chair. For his own sake, the therapist should have a few minutes' rest before the next patient arrives. Also it is wise to have an hour or two during the working day in which you can read a little, write letters, or perhaps at leisure think about countertransferences.

The period spent with the patient should be uninterrupted. This ideal is frequently violated, especially by the insistent summons of the telephone. A therapist can excuse himself, answer the call, make it as brief as possible, arrange to phone back at another time if he foresees a prolonged conversation, and apologize to the patient if the call is unavoidably long. If interruptions are handled with tact and the patient sees that you sincerely attempt to moderate them, he usually has no difficulty in understanding and accepting such reality demands.

Space Arrangements

You and the patient should work alone. At times one may see a man and wife or a parent and child in a single interview, but otherwise psychotherapy involves two people only.

The room you use is unfortunately more often determined by the financial or prestige status of the clinic than by its suitability for an interview. It is easy to take a good room for granted. A bad one introduces complications and irritants which need not be there at all. In a therapist's dreams there is a spacious, even-temperatured, quiet, well-ventilated room with friendly yielding furniture, some books, and perhaps a few pictures. In harsh reality such a set-up is enjoyed only by monetarily unembarrassed private practitioners.

Even though you may be relegated to the end of the mop closet nearest the elevator shaft, do the best you can with the help of the following thumb-and-finger rules. First, have a comfortable chair for yourself. Six or eight hours a day on one of the galley seats some clinics provide may sap your good humor. A desk need not be something to shelter one's self behind. Having the patient in a low chair and towering over him while light glares in his eyes from behind you is moviesque "corn." Also skulls, charts of the autonomic nervous system, brain models, and other medical trappings are needless props. There is no reason to feel that the room should be a bare cell "so the patient can't learn of your personal tastes and thus blur the transference." Such misguided refinements dehumanize the therapist, who after all is first a human being.

If it is at all possible, use a couch. Freud said it simply and honestly—it is unbearable to be stared at for eight hours a day. To be under constant scrutiny means that some of your energy, which should be entirely devoted to the patient's communications, is shunted into efforts to guard your facial and bodily expressions. Using a couch does not automatically mean psychoanalysis nor does it necessarily demand free association. With the patient lying down one can converse and discuss with him just as in vis-à-vis therapy. Most schizophrenics admittedly should not be placed on a couch (see Chapter 9).

Some beginners feel awkward about asking the patient to lie down. Your request understandably should not be made in the first interview. But after two or three sessions one might say, "Now today won't you lie down on this couch? It will help you to relax, and we have found that this is a convenient way to work." Most patients take to the idea easily. If the patient balks at your suggestion you might briefly discuss his objections. However, if he shows a great deal of anxiety about the prospect of lying down, allow him to remain upright and move on to another topic. Perhaps later you will discover what he is afraid of in another context.

AT the beginning of the third interview the therapist wished to shift a woman with a street phobia from sitting up to lying down.

THER. (matter-of-factly): Let's start today with you lying down over here on the couch.

PT. (startled): Any special reason?

THER. (cautiously): No, just that a couch sometimes has advantages in this sort of work.

PT. (openly upset): Well, I'd really rather not lie down if you don't mind.

THER. (with a smile): Don't mind at all. Now, last time you were telling me about your troubles at home. What's going on there these days?

The therapist intended to relieve the patient's sudden discomfort by shifting her attention and thus making psychological distance from an anxiety-laden area.

In no way make an issue out of the couch and don't give the patient a feeling that you are commanding him to lie down with an implied "or else I won't like it" threat. Like most of one's behavior in therapy, if this procedure is done quietly, smoothly, and matter-of-factly, few difficulties arise.

Having described the participants in the psychotherapeutic process and their temporal-spatial positions, let us now set them in motion and consider what goes on in their meetings.

Chapter 5

BEHAVIOR DURING THE INTERVIEW

Primarily, what the therapist wishes to take place in the interview is talking. Following our theory, you want the patient to translate his thoughts and feelings into speech which you can understand. In return, you hope to verbalize certain of your thoughts in a form which he can see as pertinent to his own. In spite of the aim to change the dynamic equilibrium of a patient's wish-defense systems entirely through the medium of speech, other modes of behavior arise both in the patient and the therapist. Before we consider what the participants in therapy say, let us discuss their actual behavior. I will make no attempt to examine in detail the motivations behind these actions, confining my remarks to ways in which they can be efficiently managed.

Behavior of the Patient

Besides what he says, the way the patient says it, with accompanying general aspect and gestures, may communicate valuable things to you. Though his entire behavior reveals lifelong character attitudes, much of what he does during the interview serves as a moment-to-moment defense against the immediate threats of the uncovering process.

For example, some hypertense patients pace up and down while talking. Hysterical characters may flamboyantly enact their thought contents as if giving a stage performance. Women patients may cross their legs seductively, while men may slouch, yawn, and hum in a transparent attempt at nonchalance. Should they impede the therapy, these defenses are handled like any others—at the right time and with an interpretation. Otherwise, they can be omitted from discussions in favor of more important topics.

More specific resistances in actions (what is defense for the patient is seen as resistance by the therapist) can be interpreted as they arise.

WHILE lying on a couch, the patient, a painfully refined woman who has had many hours of psychotherapy, falls silent after saying, "I really have nothing more to tell you about myself." After a minute or so she points to an ash-tray before her and says, "I can't stand that damn bird." (The ash-tray consists of a clay figure of a long-beaked bird.) She then arises from the couch and moves the ash-tray out of her sight. The therapist remarks, "That bird must remind you of something, and you think that by removing it from your sight you hope to rid yourself of an unpleasant thought." She agrees as to the defensive nature of her act and then confesses for the first time her great distaste for penises and anything that looks like one.

Besides moving objects in the room, the patient may treat those objects in a disclosing way, e.g., slamming the door or tearing up bits of paper into a mess for you to clean up. Too, the patient may rearrange or kick the furniture or even throw your possessions against the wall.

How permissive should one be? That the therapist is completely permissive is a polite myth. Your agreement with the patient is that he is free to say anything he pleases, not do anything he pleases. It is only a matter of common sense that the therapist, while interpreting such provocative transference behavior, as mentioned in the preceding paragraph, should tactfully forbid these actions. (A good parent must often be firm in defining limits.) Without a tone of shaming reproach, you can remind the patient of the basis of your working relationships—that he speak his thoughts rather than act them out—and frankly state that you expect him to stick to his responsibilities in this pact. Those patients having that degree of reasonable ego which fits them for psychotherapy will react favorably. With those you cannot influence in this direction, it is doubtful whether you have a workable psychotherapeutic situation.

Perhaps a more frequent problem arises when the patient, most commonly a woman, breaks down and cries. The therapist's position is simple enough—he waits until the patient is able to regain control and can go on talking about what upsets her. There is no need to say "there, there," to touch her, or to stop the interview. Since secondarily the patient, particularly if a man, may experience shame and embarrassment over his crying, you can give him a feeling that such a show of emotion is not at all disgraceful but in fact is entirely appropriate in the psychotherapeutic situation.

A MAN's father, loved and admired by the patient, is about to die. In speaking of the coming event, the patient suddenly breaks into tears and weeps freely. The therapist says nothing, waiting for the patient to partially pull himself together.

Pt. (*embarrassed and apologetic*): I'm sorry to carry on like this. It's such a stupid and childish thing.
Ther. (*kindly*): But why shouldn't you cry if something touches you? This is just the place for it.
Pt.: I guess it shows that underneath I'm a weakling.
Ther. (*delving, now that the acute burst of affect has subsided*): You mean a strong person never has deeply moving feelings?

In this manner the therapist can absolve some of the patient's shame, reinstitute the flow of material, and at the same time give the patient the feeling that he can speak of his innermost emotions without fear of humiliation.

Another behavioral problem involves the patient's request that you read something he has written about himself.

The material usually consists of an autobiography, stream-of-consciousness associations, or random reminiscences. The therapist easily recognizes the many possible defensive aspects of such behavior, e.g., to avoid talking freely, to impress the therapist with a willingness to "do something," to exhibit literary skills, to prepare the content of the interview ahead of time as insurance against surprises, etc. One approach is to have the patient read his writings aloud in the interview. Then you can deal with the content like any other of his communications and perhaps at some strategical point raise the question whether he is avoiding the free expression of his interview thoughts by the prepared writing maneuver.

Gifts (books, pictures, clothing, etc.) which the patient may bring to the therapist can also be considered as evidence of defensive purpose. The giving may have several meanings—to express love, hoping for love in return, to pacify a feared parent figure, to place the therapist in debt, etc. Whether one accepts or refuses the gift (cf. page 147), the important idea is that the therapist recognizes its transference-resistance motivation and introduces an examination of this behavior into the interview discussions. Therapists who frequently receive gifts from all sorts of patients can profitably explore in themselves the unconscious equation, gifts = love.

Behavior of the Therapist

According to the books, the therapist has only to sit, listen, and occasionally speak. Actually it is remarkable how close one can come to doing just and only that. However, a few activities are worth mention.

Sometimes a therapist may feel sleepy during an interview. To himself he owes a countertransference investiga tion and, if he dozes off, he owes an apology to the patient. The therapist can only hope that the defection will not provide too large a club for the patient's subsequent transference resistances. Other therapists have been known to pace up and down during the interview, exhorting and gesturing. It may be an impressive performance of magical inspiring, but it fails as dynamic psychotherapy.

An oft-discussed question is that of note-taking. Though taking notes during an interview may give the patient the feeling you are "doing something" and not "just sitting there," from the therapist's standpoint it has disadvantages. The main objection is that it diverts attention from what the patient is saying and from your own associations to his remarks. One cannot possibly take down everything the patient says, and in trying to select the material one does not have the time or prophetic knowledge to judge which things are the more significant. Although recorded data often give the beginner a secure feeling that in case his memory slips he has an aid, this security is false and evanescent. Clinics usually require something in the chart. As the end of the hour, after the patient has left, one can jot down a few sentences which may satisfy this demand.

By the time one has become something of a psychotherapist, his medical diagnostic judgment has suffered a disuse atrophy of such a proportion that he is really no longer a reliable medical man. This plus other well-known theoretical and practical transference reasons determines the policy that the therapist should refrain from doing physical examinations on his patients. If an examination is required before therapy, a colleague can perform it. If, during the course of therapy the patient develops symptoms which, after careful consideration, the therapist feels might have an organic basis, he can have an internist examine the patient.

Should the therapist smoke during the interview? Why not? It will help drain the small amount of undischarged tension which is always present during an interview, and it contributes to the naturalness of his behavior.

Various problems concerning etiquette may arise, particularly with women patients. Though he acts as naturally as possible during the interview, a psychotherapist must at times bypass certain chivalries, e.g., helping the patient on with her coat, picking up what she drops, and lighting her cigarettes. With men one usually shakes hands at the first meeting but not in subsequent ones. In addressing the patient by name, the prefix "Miss" or "Mrs." should be used with women. "Mr." with men is optional but it emphasizes the professional nature of the relationship and circumvents the patient's calling you by your first name.

Let us now turn to the actual experiences of psychotherapy, dividing them into a beginning period, a middle, and an end. Typical situations will be described using clinical examples from actual practice.

Chapter 6

BEGINNING THE THERAPY

Psychotherapy begins in the first interview, with the patient talking, the therapist listening. When he does speak, the therapist confines his remarks to questions and other interpositions, withholding interpretations for another time. This technique is the pivot of the initial fact-finding process around which future developments will swing. An illustrative clinical example follows:

AFTER mutual introduction, a young college girl seats herself in a chair the therapist offers.

THER.: How can I help you?
PT. (*talking rapidly*): I'm not sure myself. All I know is I've decided I've got to do something about myself. I've been reading some of those psychology books, and I can see myself on every page. I just think it would be a good idea for me to see a psychiatrist and get myself straightened out. Mother would die if she knew I was coming, because she doesn't believe in psychiatry.

EVEN though the therapist has not received an explicit categorical answer to his first question, note how immediately the patient begins to give valuable information about her relationship to her mother. Since the patient keeps talking, there is no need to interrupt at this point. She continues:

PT. (*animated*): It's not that she's old-fashioned or anything, but she just thinks everybody has problems and the only way to solve them is by leading a clean life. Get lots of sleep, take walks, and don't worry about things, she says. (*Stops.*)

40

I⊤ is not clear why the patient should suddenly stop here. Two courses are open to the therapist. He can wait in silence until the accumulation of anxiety prompts the patient to continue or he can stimulate her to go on by asking a question. Every patient has some anxiety related to talking for the first time to a psychiatrist and hence the therapist at the very beginning is more active in questioning and in encouraging the patient to talk until she can gain some ease. In this case the therapist asks a question which relates directly to the patient's last remark and which at the same time serves a direct investigative purpose:

THER.: What things do you worry about?
PT.: Well, I don't exactly worry, but things upset me. Not school, I'm doing fine there. To be honest about it, I guess it's boy friends. I can't seem to hang on to one very long, and I always wind up being hurt. Then I get in a tizzy and get all upset.
THER.: What happens to you?

THE patient then describes anxiety symptoms of palpitation, severe restlessness, nausea and occasional vomiting which she has suffered for several months. They precede and follow dates with boys to whom she is attracted but who she fears will lose interest in her and not return. The therapist asks a few questions about the onset and details of these symptoms. In doing so, he notices that the patient is making shorter and shorter answers, limiting herself to the topic of the question and waiting for the next question from the therapist to provide her specific material. The therapist, to avoid accustoming the patient to the idea that psychotherapeutic interviews are solely a question-answer process, tosses the ball back to her by asking a general question which prompts her to be responsible for selecting the topic.

THER.: And what else is bothering you?
PT. (after a pause): I don't know how important it is, but in the last few years I've been having trouble with my mother. It seems we're always arguing about something or other. Like today, she was giving me a bad time about coming in late last night. She thinks a girl should be home and in bed by eleven o'clock. You'd think I'd committed a crime the way she

carries on when I come home late. With her nagging at me on top of vomiting all night, sometimes I think I'm going crazy. (*Visibly upset, weeps.*) Do I sound crazy?

FRIGHTENED and in a turmoil she seeks support from an authoritative source or parent-figure. The portion of a patient's ego participating in the therapeutic interview consists of an observing and an experiencing component, the former reporting on, and at times stepping back to evaluate, the latter. When the experiencing component becomes flooded with affect and thus expands to overrun the observing component, direct reassurance by words and manner should be given to alleviate the patient's distressing feelings and to provide room for the renewed participation of the observing component. Hence, as is characteristic for initial interviews, the therapist interposes by giving what the patient seeks at the moment and then shifts the discussion away from the affect-flooding topic of mother:

THER. (*sincere, definite*): Not at all. This sounds like a common enough problem between most mothers and daughters—the old battle between generations. Now you mentioned boy friends. Do you have a boy friend currently?

PT. (*somewhat relieved*): Yes, I've been going steady now with a fellow for about two months.

THER.: Is he a student too?

PT.: He's a chem major. He's graduating this year, and then he's going to grad school.

THER. (*again asking a general question to give the patient free rein*): What's he like?

PT. (*faint smile*): He's very intelligent. And a good sense of humor. I wouldn't call him handsome, but he's not bad. His name is George. We like the same things, books and concerts. He has a car, and we go for long drives into the country when he gets off his job on the night shift.

SHE goes on at some length about the activities they share and their common interests. Now that the patient has regained some measure of control of her emotions and is reporting freely, the therapist can again attempt an approach to the loaded topic of late hours and mother. Of course, if he had sensed that the patient was still so shaken that such a move would produce another emotional upheaval, he would postpone the attempt until later, perhaps even until the next interview.

THER.: And it's these dates with George that keep you out late?
PT. (*now able to speak more calmly*): Yes. When we go for drives I get home about one or two o'clock. Mother hears me come in, I guess, and then the fireworks start the next morning. She's all questions—"What did you do? Where did you go? Why can't you get home earlier?" and so forth.
HER.: She knows George?
PT.: Oh, yes. I've had him to the house for dinner a couple of times. I think she likes him all right. I don't know why she worries so. I mean about being out late.

In this manner the psychotherapeutic interview proceeds —the therapist for the most part listening, occasionally questioning, and at times taking active steps to stem the overflow of affects which distress the patient and interrupt the fact-finding process. During the first one or two interviews the therapist has two aims: (a) to formulate from the facts gathered a working clinical and dynamic diagnosis and (b) to acclimatize the patient to the interview methods and procedure of psychotherapeutic work. The first aim determines the suitability of the patient for therapy and roughly the type of therapy which will be undertaken, i.e., mainly covering or mainly uncovering. The second aim has the more long-range goal of preparing the patient for the roles he and the therapist will take in future meetings. Let us now consider the problem of diagnosis and later the aspects of educating the patient.

Diagnosing the Disorder

To establish a *clinical diagnosis* we utilize psychiatric knowledge of symptomatology and personality structure in deciding first whether the patient's difficulties result from an organic, a psychotic, or a neurotic process. If the therapist feels that there might be an organic disease present, the patient is first examined by an internist or neurologist before any plans for psychotherapy are considered. If the patient is psychotic, one may wish to make other arrangements for him, or one may feel that his ego functions possess sufficient reality sense to make him suitable for psychotherapy. (cf. Chapter 9.) The diagnosis of neurosis can be further though not sharply subdivided into the usual categories, anxiety hysterias, obsessive-compulsive states, depressions, etc. Suitability for psychotherapy is not so much determined by the clinical label as by the factors discussed in Chapter 2 and by the dynamic diagnosis.

A *dynamic diagnosis* consists of an evaluation of the patient's current dominant neurotic conflicts, of those ego areas failing to cope with the resultant disturbance and of the intact ego functions attempting to reinstate an equilibrium. The formulation of the neurosis in terms of decompensating and compensating ego processes serves as a guide for therapy in selecting what aspects of the patient's personality will be touched and whether mainly covering or uncovering maneuvers will be attempted. A few clinical examples follow to illustrate dynamic diagnoses.

1. AN unmarried girl for the preceding three years has suffered acute anxiety symptoms preceding and sometimes during dates with boy friends. The symptoms have been of the same intensity until a few months previous to the interview, when they became markedly worse for no apparent reason. At other moments in her life she has no difficulty. She holds a responsible job, has many friends, and takes an interest in social affairs.

She had grown up in an atmosphere filled with the shouts of arguing parents, who were finally divorced when she was twelve. From then on she lived with her mother, who missed no opportunity to warn her of men's sexual greed and animal nature. Despite this indoctrination, the patient in adolescence became interested in boys and went through several secret crushes. During college years, when she was away from home, her symptoms began on her first solo date. Since then she has had many dates with different boys without amelioration of her fears.

As a person she is intelligent, efficient, and businesslike. She is overscrupulous about her personal appearance, becoming upset if a wisp of hair is out of place or her dress develops a wrinkle. Her friends tell her not to be so demanding in regard to punctuality, and they "kid" her about her rigid scheduling of all activities in both work and play. To her these qualities are not at all bothersome, in fact she is sure she would not like to be any other way.

The clinical diagnosis for this patient was anxiety neurosis in a moderately compulsive character. The dynamic diagnosis indicated the predominant conflict as centering around her sexual orientation to men. Though there was failure of her ego defenses in this area, the remaining areas seemed well compensated by reaction formations and other mechanisms. In therapy an approach would be made into the sphere of male relationships, leaving untouched her ego-syntonic compulsive character structure.

2. AFTER serving for years as the mistress of a married man, a middle-aged secretary has become depressed when he finally said he could not marry her and returned to his wife. Symptoms of depression have continued for four years, with the patient losing interest in other men, hoping that one day her lover would return. This hope has been kept alive by correspondence with the man, who still likes her but feels that his first duty is to his wife and children. However, she realizes that her life cannot go on in this way, that she must seek new experiences if she is ever to marry.

Her childhood and adolescence had been characterized by a vigorous tomboyishness in an attempt to please both her father and her mother, who placed a premium on ruggedness and courage. In school she had competed successfully with boys academically as well as athletically. Only men who could outdistance her in every respect had had an appeal for her. She had met few of this type in her adult life until the married man who had had the affair with her.

In appearance she is quite feminine and alert. Though she often weeps, a smile at times shows up. She expresses no bitterness toward the man who left her; in fact she seems to admire him for his loyalty to his wife.

Clinically the picture is that of a neurotic depression. Dynamically the patient's conflict relates to the loss of a prized love-object, with a subsequent reversal of the repressed hostility. Instead of making a masculine identification to compensate for what she in childhood assumed to be a defect, she was seeking a certain type of man to increment her status. Therapy would first attempt to relieve the depressive symptoms by working in the sector of her reaction to the loss. Only much later, if the first maneuvers were unsuccessful, would a more extensive investigation of her conditions for love be considered.

3. A WEEK before coming to therapy, a thirty-eight-year-old man had been discharged from the hospital after spending three months in recovering from an acute psychotic episode. His psychiatrist at the hospital had advised him to receive psychotherapy, and the patient is eager to prevent another breakdown. His memory of his thoughts and behavior in the episode is vague, but laughingly he recalls one belief that he was Jesus Christ. In the hospital, another patient had interested him in a metaphysical cult whose ideas he feels are of great help to him.

Both parents had died while he was an infant, and he was raised by a grandmother until he was sixteen, when he began to support himself as a professional musician. As far back as he can remember he has been homosexual. All his affairs with men have ended after one or two experiences. He takes the passive role in the sex acts and enjoys the feeling of doing something for someone. He has no conscious conflict about his homosexuality, believing that it is the preferred way of life for a musician who is never in one place very long. His main interest is in philosophy and in systems of thought which explain the way in which people and the world behave.

The clinical diagnosis is schizophrenia. In a psychosis of this degree, with the shattering of multiple ego areas, it is difficult to isolate a predominating conflict, since so many wish-defense systems show severe disturbance. Certainly the patient's delusion and homosexuality point to his difficulties in a role as a man toward other men. If therapy (mainly covering; cf. Chapter 9) should be attempted in this case, it would cautiously endeavor to take advantage of his ego mechanism of intellectualization by encouraging his already roused interest in a religion, cult, or philosophical theory.

Acceptance and Declination

Upon establishing, usually after the first or second interview, working clinical and dynamic diagnosis along with an estimate of the patient's suitability for psychotherapy, the therapist proceeds to plan his future moves. Some patients he will at once decline to treat, some he will see for only a few interviews, and some he will select to treat for weeks or months.

Accepting a patient for psychotherapy presents few problems. Once the therapist decides to treat the patient, he makes some statement to the effect that he is interested in trying to help and outlines his plan as to appointments, hours, etc. An important principle at this point is that *the therapist does not promise the patient a cure.* In all honesty he cannot and should not make such a prediction. A psychotherapeutic working agreement is made on the basis that the therapist doesn't know yet whether he can relieve the patient but that he feels it is worth the effort to make an attempt. An example follows:

DURING the initial interviews a young artist whom the therapist intends to treat for a work inhibition asks:

Pr.: From what you know so far, do you think you can get me over this inhibition?

THER. (*speculative but confident*): Oh, that would be hard to say definitely. Let's just work together for a while and see how it goes.

Pr. (*wanting some assurance*): But you think there's a chance?

THER.: That I do. We agree the trouble is psychological, you want therapy, I'm interested in trying to help you. So let's start in with your painting. When did you begin painting?

The frequency of the interviews depends on factors in each individual case. Therapy which is mainly uncovering (dissolving defenses) requires interviews twice or even three times a week. Supportive and covering therapy (increasing defenses) can be accomplished at once-a-week or even less frequent intervals. As for the total duration of therapy, again such a prediction cannot reliably be made. The inquisitive patient is simply told this truth. Certain patients can be advised in general terms that therapy will be a long haul. For example:

SINCE the age of five a young man has suffered severe stammering. After trying all sorts of schools and speech methods, he seeks psychotherapeutic help. Intelligent, witty and of vigorous drive, he is eager to tackle and overcome his handicap quickly. However, the therapist realizes from other experiences that such problems require long and intensive effort.

Pr.: How long do you think it will take before there are any results?

THER.: That's impossible to say. We'll have to see how it goes as we go along. But you should understand that it will be a matter of months and maybe even a few years. Don't let that discourage you. It's just that these things aren't solved in an hour or a week.

If the therapist is working in a clinic or on a service he plans to leave in a few weeks or months, he must in all fairness to the patient inform him of this fact when accepting him for therapy. Springing the news of departure two weeks before the event may be an unthinkingly cruel blow to the patient and needlessly complicate the work of the next therapist.

Declining those patients who the therapist feels are not suitable for therapy may involve a variety of procedures. One is for the therapist to take the side of whatever conscious resistances the patient has to consulting a psychiatrist, as in the following examples:

1. A SULLEN and effeminate-looking man is referred by his physician after a routine physical examination. He sits silently and waits for the therapist to speak.

THER.: And what brings you to see me?
PT. (somewhat annoyed): I don't know. Dr. S. just told me I should see you.
THER. (acting puzzled): But what for?
PT.: I don't know. You'll have to ask him.
THER.: What did you see him for?

THE patient then gives an account of the physical examination he has taken in the process of obtaining a job in a restaurant. During the examination the physician has asked him if he is homosexual. He has affirmed this and been told flatly he should see a psychiatrist to get straightened out. He has obeyed the command, in order not to displease the physician and perhaps jeopardize his chance for the job.

THER.: But as far as you are concerned, unless you had been told to, you wouldn't have consulted a psychiatrist?
PT.: That's right. I don't think I need a psychiatrist. I'm all right the way I am.
THER.: Well, I don't see any reason why you should come either. You're getting along all right. Why don't we leave it this way, that if anything comes up that bothers you, you can give me a ring? Otherwise let's let it go.

Pt. (*smiles with relief*): Okay by me. Thanks very much.
Ther. (*getting up*): You're welcome. Goodbye.

It was obvious from the patient's initial interview manner and appearance and from his referral story that he had a conscious unwillingness to see a psychiatrist. He wanted to keep his homosexuality intact. This was sufficient to make him at that time unsuitable for therapy. Hence the therapist simply agreed with the strong resistances and the declination was effected.

2. For many years a woman patient has moved from one mystical cult or esthetic fad to another in an effort to find a viewpoint which would explain the meaning of life. Recently she has read of psychiatry and wondered if here she might fulfil her search. Also a friend has told her that she is neurotic and should see a psychiatrist.

Ther.: And do you agree with your friend?
Pt. (*a little ruffled*): No, I don't think I'm any more neurotic than anyone else. She's the one who ought to see a psychiatrist. My idea was only to learn more about psychiatry at first hand and compare it with semantics.
Ther.: It's really not my function to instruct people in psychiatry. My job is to treat people who are psychologically ill or upset. And this doesn't seem to be the case as far as you are concerned.
Pt.: I don't think I'm mentally sick if that's what you mean. I'm not so much interested in the treatment in psychiatry as in its philosophy, what it stands for.
Ther. (*frankly*): I couldn't be of much help to you that way. Your best bet would be to go to the various lectures being given around town and read some of the books on the subject.
Pt.: Where could I find out about them?
Ther.: Oh, you might try the Medical Center or get in touch with the Mental Health Society.

This patient's goal was not that of psychotherapy but of instruction. Her openly expressed resistance to the idea of psychotherapy was capitalized on in declining her for future treatment.

In cases such as the two just mentioned, the beginning psychotherapist should beware of trying to convince the patient that he needs therapy. It is a mistake, often a disastrous one, to break the patient down by showing him how badly off he is and thus frighten him into therapy. Also unwise is the attempt to lure the patient into treatment by promising him he will feel much better or get along with people more easily. Though there may be obvious clinical signs of a neurotic or psychotic disturbance in the patient, our knowledge of the personality as a labile equilibrium of checking and balancing wish-defense forces should correctly warn us often to leave well enough alone.

It may be more difficult to decline a patient unsuitable for psychotherapy who has no conscious resistances to treatment and who eagerly seeks help. Each case is an individual problem depending on its unique circumstances. Below are some examples.

1. BECAUSE he plans to marry a young woman who insists that he first overcome a sexual impotence, a fifty-five-year-old man applies for help. He is intelligent, successful in his career and eager to do anything to prove to his fiancée that he will make a suitable husband. Impotent since his first attempt at intercourse at fifteen, he has always accepted it as an inevitable part of his nature. Though he has seldom felt much sexual desire, he has tried intercourse a few times in his life but has never been able to produce an erection. This handicap seemingly does not trouble him greatly, since he feels that the true test of a man comes in the business world, where he had proved himself more than adequate. Why he should decide to marry at this time is not yet clear.

His personality is that of a rigid and domineering compulsive character with extensive reaction formations and isolations. These defensive systems maintain his ego in excellent compensation, the only major symptom apparently being the sexual impotence.

The therapist feels that there is little hope of curing a forty-year symptom imbedded in such an inflexible personality structure and that it would be futile to attempt to dismantle such otherwise successful defenses. One possibility for therapy might be his decision to marry.

THER.: I really don't feel there is much chance of modifying your impotence. It's gone on for so many years now that it's pretty well fixed.

PT. (*disappointed*): I can see what you mean, but I want to get married and she won't have me unless we can have intercourse.

THER.: How is it that you've been unmarried all these years and now you suddenly decide to get married?

THE patient with some hesitance tells of meeting his fiancée, a girl of twenty, in a bar about two months before. His friends tell him he is crazy to marry her, that she is after his money. He rejects this opinion, is determined to marry her, and even dismisses the therapist's remarks that he might want to discuss his decision further.

THER.: Well, I'm sorry I can't help you with the sexual problem. You might have some conflict over marrying this girl that we could work on but you say not.

PT.: No, I have no conflict. If you can't help the impotence, then I'll have to try something else.

THER.: Okay. Sorry I can't be of help.

2. WHEN crossed by her husband, a woman patient who is no longer young has developed acute anxiety attacks over a period of twenty years. During these spells she shrieks and moans, chokes up, fears she is going to die, and has violent heart poundings. After a small dose of phenobarbital and a few hours of solicitous bed care by the husband, she recovers completely. Her accusations that he has caused the attack by arguing with her produce sufficient guilt in her husband that he grants her some favor or gift. Although she is treated by her physician and hus-

band as if she had heart attacks, she has always secretly recognized that these disturbances were psychological. A sister has convinced the patient that her attacks are psychological and has recommended psychotherapy.

After two interviews the therapist has gathered sufficient information to form the opinion that the patient is unsuitable for therapy. The secondary gains of the neurosis, an infantile personality, and a lack of psychological-mindedness combine to make the prognosis poor.

THER. (*doubting but not definite*): I'm not sure this kind of treatment will help you.

PT. (*protesting*): But don't you think that my trouble is psychological?

THER. (*agreeable*): Oh, yes. I agree with you on that, but I'm wondering if psychotherapy will relieve you.

PT.: Why won't it?

THER. (*now definite*): Well, there are several factors. First, your condition has been going on for a long time now, and it wouldn't be easy to get rid of. Then, this sort of problem takes weeks and months of work, and my feeling is that after a year we wouldn't be much closer to the root of your difficulty.

PT. (*upset*): But what am I going to do? I can't go on this way.

THER. (*reassuring*): Still, I think you do pretty well with these spells. You can get them under control with your medicine, and they soon pass. One suggestion I would have would be about these arguments with your husband. Maybe you could work on getting along with him and not let his stubbornness upset you. When you see an argument coming up, take a walk along the beach or go for a drive by yourself until you can cool down.

This simple advice was not given with the aim of changing her neurosis but (a) to reassure her that hers was not a hopeless situation and (b) to give her something to work on by herself by prescribing activities known to provide discharges of aggression and hostility. A psychotherapist must at times see clearly and admit to himself that there are irreversible psychological conditions which he can do little about.

3. A DEPRESSED and mildly paranoid woman of modest intelligence wants help for her spells of gloominess and lack of interest. Her symptoms developed suddenly three weeks previously when her room-mate moved out to get married. As she looks around the apartment, happy memories of the room-mate crop up, accentuating her present loneliness. Though in the acute stage of a reactive depression, she does not appear suicidal. Her limited intellect and underlying psychosis influence the therapist to decline her for psychotherapy.

In the history he has noted that the patient has an older sister who has guided and comforted her in the past. Attempting (a) to get the patient away for a while from the actual scene which revives memories of the room-mate and (b) to provide a substitute source of a mother-child relationship, the therapist directs the discussion toward the sister.

THER.: At present I think what you need is to get away from here for a while. Didn't you say your sister lived in Los Angeles?
PT.: Right near there.
THER.: Why not go down and stay with her until you feel a little better?
PT.: I've thought of it but I'm not sure. She invited me to spend my vacation with her.
THER.: I'd go there. It will help you forget this trouble. In different surroundings you'll soon get some of your energy back.

Thus in declining to attempt psychotherapy with certain patients, it is often possible with the exercise of some resourcefulness to recommend environmental changes or to offer sensible advice. However, these suggestions should not relate to major decisions such as divorce, having a baby, giving up a career, etc. If the therapist wishes to advise on such matters, he should have much more data than can be gathered in one or two interviews.

The Patient Learns

Previously I mentioned a second goal involved in the technique of the early interviews, i.e., accustoming the patient to the therapist's manner of working. This aspect of psychotherapy begins with the first meeting. If it is introduced correctly, the patient does not notice much difference between the therapist's role in the first diagnostic interviews and in the later hours of more specific therapy. The therapist may be slightly more active in questioning and in showing interest at first, later becoming more of the quiet observer. Thus there is an easy transition from the initial diagnostic goal to the long-range goal of modifying neurotic conflicts.

Once the patient is being seen regularly, he soon learns many of the therapist's everyday methods and tactics. An important one concerns the situation when the patient falls silent. The therapist usually does one of three things: (a) asks him what he's thinking about, (b) asks him some other direct question, or (c) simply waits for him to continue. The principle underlying the therapist's choice among these devices will be discussed later (cf. page 103). Clinical examples of the three techniques follow:

Inquiring About Unspoken Thoughts.

THE patient opens the interview with a few random details about what she has been doing the past few days, buying clothes, sunbathing, etc. She then stops talking. The therapist waits about ten seconds and then interrupts the silence.

THER. (encouragingly): Just say what you're thinking about.
PT.: I'm not thinking about much of anything. (Pause.)
THER.: Say whatever comes into your mind.
PT. (laughs): My mind is really a blank.

THER.: It may seem that way to you at first, but there are always some thoughts there. Just as your heart is always beating, there's always some thought or other going through your mind.

PT.: Your mentioning the word "heart" reminds me that the doctor told my mother the other day she had a weak heart.

AND she begins to talk freely again. There is no discussion of the resistance involved (cf. page 95). As this point the therapist only offers an explanation to acquaint the patient with his wish that she report the thoughts which occur to her during the interview.

In another interview the same patient again becomes silent and the therapist repeats his encouragement.

THER.: Just say what comes to you.

PT.: Oh, odds and ends that aren't very important.

THER.: Say them anyway.

PT.: I don't see how they could have much bearing. I was wondering what sort of books those are over there. But that hasn't anything to do with what I'm here for.

THER.: One never can tell, and actually you're in no position to judge what has bearing and what hasn't. Let me decide that. You just report what comes into your mind regardless of whether you think it's important or not.

Here the therapist has taught the patient a little "free" association, instructing her not to censor or dismiss thoughts. He knows that there is always some censorship taking place in every patient, and his aim is not to completely eradicate it but to accustom the patient to her responsibility of continuously providing material for his examination and consideration.

Asking a Direct Question.—The question relates to some topic other than the silence. This device requires little illustration.

AFTER talking at length about his father's death a few years ago, the patient stops.

Pt.: I guess that's about all there is to it.

Ther. (*after a short wait*): And then what did your mother do for a living?

The patient learns that at times the therapist does interrupt a silence to gather information on some point which interests him.

Waiting for the Patient to Continue.—This technique, the patient soon discovers, is the psychotherapist's stock-in-trade. In contrast to social conversations, the therapist does not seem to be made ill at ease by a silence. This may puzzle or annoy patients, particularly those who equate the therapist's words with his interest.

During the third interview a woman falls silent. The therapist waits quietly for her to continue. She acts as if she were waiting for him to speak, and when he does not she becomes curious.

Pt.: Why don't you say something?

Ther.: I'm waiting to hear what your next thoughts are.

Pt.: What I'm wondering is why you don't talk more.

Ther.: I have to know a great deal about you before I can say anything that will be of help. So my job is to listen while you do most of the talking. Don't worry, when the time comes, I'll talk.

Another situation where the therapist is more frequently silent occurs at the beginning of each interview. One waits for the patient to begin with whatever topic he chooses, and then his lead is followed. If he is silent at the start, after a short wait the therapist can ask him what he is thinking about. Anxious or depressed patients may be somewhat inarticulate in the early stages of therapy, and with them one must patiently adjust to their slow pace while encouraging them to keep on voicing their thoughts.

When the patient becomes silent and notes that the therapist remains silent also, he may attempt to ease his tension by asking a question which prompts the therapist to speak.

At times the therapist answers, but often he does not. Not receiving an answer to a direct question may confuse or irritate a patient used to the give-and-take of ordinary conversation.

SEEING that the therapist is not going to break the silence of the past many seconds, a lively and intense matron poses an interesting question.

PT.: I've often wondered why anyone would go into this business. Tell me, how did you get interested in psychiatry?

IN this particular case the therapist wishes to do two things at this point: (a) introduce to the patient the idea that questions are dealt with like any other material in the interview and not necessarily answered and (b) open up the area of the patient's transference thoughts which he feels might be at the root of her resistance to talking. He waits and says nothing.

PT. (a little affronted by the seeming impoliteness): Why don't you answer? Isn't that a reasonable question?
THER. (agreeably): It is. But this isn't a question-and-answer process. If your thoughts come to you in the form of questions, we look on them as any other thoughts. This doesn't mean you shouldn't ask questions if they are on your mind, but I don't guarantee to answer them. For instance, in this case it seems that what is on your mind are some thoughts about me.
PT. (accepting the explanation): That's right. I do wonder about you. You don't seem the sort of person I'd expect to find being a psychiatrist.
THER.: Why not?

Psychodynamic Role of the Patient's Questions.—Before discussing further the technical problem of handling questions directed to the therapist, we must briefly consider the psychodynamic role of these questions in the interview. In the case cited above, for example, the patient's question was a defensive attempt to avoid talking about her feelings toward the therapist by making him talk instead. To perceive the dynamic function of a question, the therapist must (a) note the time when it arises and (b) look beyond the face value of the actual word content. Here are examples to show some underlying meanings questions may have.

1. THE mother of two small boys begins the hour with an account of how their perpetual activity and bickering rivalry run her ragged. She has read all sorts of books and tried all sorts of tricks, but she can't seem to relieve the drain on herself. The boys run to her for every little need, and each constantly complains about the injustices suffered at the hands of the other.

As she proceeds to elaborate on how she attempts to settle arguments between her sons, she speaks more hesitantly as if a little embarrassed. Finally, with some reluctance and expressed guilt, she admits that she secretly favors the younger boy because he is more obedient and friendly. One of her child psychology books states that one sibling should not be favored over another and she asks for corroboration from the therapist.

PT.: That's true, isn't it, that a child can be emotionally harmed by being given less affection than his brother?

HERE the manifest question concerns an opinion on child development. But the question behind the question relates to the patient as a mother. At the moment, experiencing the sting of her verbalized guilt feelings, she is really asking the therapist, "Do you think I'm a bad mother for favoring one of my sons over the other?" The therapist can then choose, depending on what he wishes to accomplish at the moment, and where the patient is in therapy, which of the two questions (the manifest or implied) he will deal with.

Answering the direct question could take the form:

THER.: Sometimes yes and sometimes no. One never can divide something like affections into exactly equal portions anyway. What do you notice in the older boy that worries you?

OR handling the implied question by bringing it out into the open could be phrased:

THER.: What you are really asking is, "Am I a bad person for favoring the younger boy?"

2. A SUPERIOR physics student is being treated for a marital problem. He and his wife repeatedly engage in fierce arguments over political, esthetic, or philosophical questions. All his life he has been a very argumentative person and has enjoyed it, but now his wife threatens to leave him unless he tempers his combativeness. Also in college he is getting into difficulties with his professors by challenging their opinions. One of them has even told him that he is overly aggressive and should see a psychiatrist about it.

From the beginning and for several interviews the patient has been friendly and eagerly cooperative, perhaps even a little over-compliant. He comes early for his appointments, calls the therapist "sir," and often apologizes for the irrelevance of the material he presents. In this interview he begins to talk of his interest in the field of psychology. He has read and discussed the subject a great deal with friends. Once he has considered changing his major from physics to psychology. However, he finds he cannot agree with many of the concepts in psychology, especially those of a psychoanalytic nature. He asks:

PT.: Take the unconscious mind, for example. What do you believe? Do you think there is really an unconscious?

THE face value of the question concerns the validity of a scientific concept. Its true psychological meaning concerns the patient's relationship to the therapist. We see in this intellectualized provocativeness the beginning emergence of the patient's competitiveness with the therapist. Cautious at first, he is now sounding out his rival's ground in preparation for the eventual struggle so typical for his personality.

3. A COMBAT veteran one day begins the hour by asking the therapist at what ages cancer occurs. Offhand the therapist cannot in his own mind connect the manifest question with anything specific he knows about the patient and hence cannot immediately arrive at the implied question. He proceeds:

THER.: Cancers occur at all ages, but mostly in older people. Why do you ask?

Pt.: My mother wrote me last week that a friend of mine, only thirty-eight, died of cancer. We grew up together and were in the army overseas together. A swell guy. It seemed awfully young to me to be dying from cancer. She said he had a cancer of the intestines.

Now the therapist suddenly recalls that for many months after his discharge from the army, the patient suffered symptoms of a recurrent amoebic dysentery. Occasionally nowadays he has slight diarrhea. Behind the request for factual information, perhaps he has a fear that he has or will get cancer.

Ther.: Have your bowels been acting up recently?
Pt.: Not especially. But you're on the right track. When I had that dysentery, I used to think maybe I had cancer. Sometimes nowadays when I get an ache or pain, it flashes into my mind: "Maybe I've got a cancer."

The implied question, guessable but obscure at first, now becomes clear. He is really asking, "Could I have cancer at my age?"

Returning to the therapist's ways of handling questions which become familiar to the patient, it is obvious that the therapist shows elasticity, at one time answering the manifest question, at another time remaining silent or touching on the implied question. Speaking generally, in a mainly uncovering therapy the therapist is more often silent or refers to the implied question while in supportive or covering therapy direct questions are more often answered or dodged. An example of the latter follows:

It is characteristic for this determined though phobic school teacher to flood the interview hour with a Niagara of direct questions. As therapy has proceeded, she has become accustomed to having a few of them unanswered, but she insists on responses to the majority of them. The therapist has learned that unless her desires are followed in this respect, she feels mistreated and lapses into an angry silence which is difficult to overcome. Wishing to avoid these silence barriers, the therapist answers and dodges until he can direct the discussion into other channels.

PT.: And then I worry about getting pregnant. You're a doctor, you should know whether a diaphragm is safe. Do you think I have reason to worry?

THER.: From all that I know a diaphragm is supposed to be the best contraceptive. But I'm really no authority on these things.

PT. (*rushing on*): Well, could someone get pregnant even when they used a diaphragm? Supposing it didn't fit any more? Are you sure a diaphragm is all right?

THER.: No, don't take my opinion as the most reliable one. If you have all these doubts, why don't you see your regular doctor?

PT. (*ignoring advice*): Why can't you tell me? This isn't a silly fear like some of my other ones. You know once I did get pregnant and had to have an abortion. Boy, that was a rough time, I don't want to go through that again.

THER. (*quickly*): What happened?

THE therapist sees a chance to switch the patient's attention to a historical event, thus escaping temporarily from the barrage of questions and also exploring some of the patient's past experiences connected with her pregnancy fears.

Handling Personal Questions.—One type of direct question the patient may learn to give up (again there are always exceptions) is that referring to the therapist's private life. In this area perhaps more than any other, the therapist, wishing to allow transferences to develop on a minimum factual basis, is silent or evasive. However, beginners in psychotherapy often have difficulty in gracefully meeting such direct personal questions. For that reason the more common personal questions and possible ways of handling them are listed below. As with other questions, the therapist first takes note of their timing and of their underlying implication.

Age. Patients often are curious about the therapist's age, especially if he appears younger than they. Thus a typical question early in therapy is:

Pt.: Doctor, how old are you?

Again we have (a) the manifest question requiring a numerical answer and (b) the implied question requiring some statement as to the therapist's experience. Suggested answers are:

a) Ther.: Twenty-eight. (*Waits for the patient's response— disappointment or satisfaction.*)
b) Ther.: Old enough to assure you you won't be a guinea-pig. [or] Perhaps you're worried about whether I've had enough experience to treat you.

With personal questions the therapist may decide simply to answer a few of them and then wait to see what the patient's next remark will concern, as in the next category.

Training. As in the situation with age, the patient is often asking about your ability to help him or measuring you by the places you have been:

Pt.: Where are you from, doctor?
Ther.: Chicago.
Pt.: Is that where you went to school?
Ther.: No. I went to college and medical school in New York.
Pt.: And where did you get your psychiatric training?
Ther.: In Boston and here in San Francisco. But it seems you are very curious about my background. Why do you think that is?
Pt.: I guess I want to make sure I'm in good hands. My father once had a doctor who knew from nothing and as a result now one of his legs is shorter than the other.
Ther.: How did all that happen?

Here we see that an important event in the patient's life is connected with his question.

Marital Status. A favorite question of woman patients who consciously or unconsciously see the therapist as a potential mate is the following:

PT.: Are you married?
THER.: Why do you ask?
PT.: Just curious. You don't have to answer if you don't want to. (*After the therapist remains silent.*) My guess is you're not married. Because if you were you'd say so. Since you're being defensive about it, it means you're not married, but afraid to say so.
THER.: And if I'm not married, what then?
PT.: Oh, then I begin to wonder why not. Maybe you're shy with women. Or maybe some woman gave you a bad time.

IT is noteworthy in this example that the therapist in reality is married but allows the patient to continue her guess that he isn't in order to investigate her subsequent transference fantasies.

Political or Religious Beliefs. Patients often want as a therapist someone whose opinions in political and religious matters come close to their own. If the therapist is like them, they feel strengthened and reassured. If not, they may use the difference to block or interrupt the therapy.

PT.: Now before we go any further with these treatments, doctor, I'd like to know whether you believe there is a God.
THER.: Why?
PT.: As I've told you, I'm an Adventist, and I wouldn't feel right about bringing my troubles to a psychiatrist who's an atheist. I don't care what your religion is as long as you're not Godless. Just tell me if you believe in God, in a Supreme Being.
THER. (*candidly*): No, I don't.
PT.: Well, then, I have no choice but to see someone else. Is that all right with you?
THER.: Sure, in fact I think it would be better for you to see someone you had more confidence in.

In such situations, infrequent as they are, the therapist comes to a point where he must face the issue of the direct question, answer it, and await the consequences.

How Patient Regards the Therapist's Questions.— While on the subject of questions, let us consider how some of the questions the therapist asks may ring in the patient's mind. When the therapist poses a question, two sets of ideas often occur to the patient. First are those thoughts which specifically answer the question and second, wonderings about why that particular question is asked at this time, i.e., what line of thought the therapist is taking. This line of thought, once understood, becomes very important for the patient because he assumes (and by and large correctly) that this direction is psychotherapeutically a worth-while one, promising in the long run relief of symptoms or an increased understanding of himself.

1. A LIVELY young woman is being treated for an obsessional murderous thought and frequent migrainous headaches. In the third interview she has spent much of the time describing events of the week end. Saturday she lunched with friends and spent the afternoon shopping. That evening she went to a party but soon after arriving noticed the typical beginning of a headache. It didn't turn out to be very severe and was gone by the following morning.

She then changes the subject to her plans for the following week end, when she intends to go to the mountains. As she prepares to describe this trip, the therapist interrupts:

THER.: You mentioned a few minutes ago that Saturday after noon you felt fine, but at the party in the evening you had a headache. Tell me what happened between those times.
PT.: Nothing special that I can think of. I went home, talked to my girl friend for awhile, got dressed. Oh, yeah. Here's something. Jack was late in picking me up that night, and we had a squabble about that.
THER.: Could you enlarge on the squabble? Give me the details.

By the use of interpositions the therapist focuses attention on an interval between states of well-being and a pain, with the implication that perhaps something occurred which could be connected with the development of her headache. Once a significant event is discovered, he holds the patient in this area by showing interest in it and requesting further information.

2. THE therapist knows that a major childhood experience of an intelligent though wayward adolescent boy was the death of his father when the patient was eight. In the fifth interview the patient describes his feelings of inferiority in competitive sports, especially baseball, which his friends play and follow enthusiastically. He is puzzled about the lack of ability, because in other physical activities he is well coordinated. His main difficulty in baseball is ball-shyness, fearing a hard ball coming directly at him. As far back as he can remember, he was frightened of a ball approaching him. The therapist asks:

THER.: As a boy, did you play catch with your father?

THOUGH at first this might seem to the patient to be an irrelevant question, it is of a nature which will arouse his curiosity as to what the therapist is driving at. Evidently the therapist by his question is linking "father" with "ball fear." The question implies, "Let's look here, maybe we will find something to help you."

The Psychotherapeutic Atmosphere.—Finally, the way questions, both those of the patient and those of the therapist, are handled in the interviews gives psychotherapy an atmosphere unique in human relationships. The patient gradually learns that his therapist is interested in examining and studying his mental processes without formulating whether they are good or bad, right or wrong, normal or abnormal. Even though in his own mind the therapist may deem some thought or behavior as psychopathological, he seldom says so, realizing how often nowadays "neurotic" means "bad" and that because "bad" means punishment, it is hidden or censored. The therapist wants the patient to present as much as possible about all of his thoughts and behavior and not select them for scrutiny on the basis of his own value systems.

IN the beginning of therapy a housewife mentions that she does not like to stay at home alone at night. If her husband is away for a few hours, she visits friends or has friends visit her. Too, if she must be alone in the house she makes sure that the doors and windows are locked. This problem interests the therapist, who wishes to explore it further but meets resistance phrased in a manner common among contemporary patients.

THER.: And what do you feel it is that makes you uneasy when you're alone?

PT. (evasive): I don't know. Some sort of vague anxiety.

THER.: But about what?

PT.: Well, that someone might break in.

THER.: A man?

PT. (lightly): Sure, that's it. But I don't see anything abnormal about that. All the women I know don't like to be alone at night. I don't think I'm different from anybody else in that respect.

THER. (explaining): But you see, here we're not interested in whether it's normal or abnormal, common or uncommon. We're trying to understand how your mind works, regardless of whether it's like others or not. For instance, sure, lots of women have this fear, but let's see what it means to you. What are you afraid will happen if a man breaks in?

THIS patient makes a division between what is normal (like others) and what is neurotic (unique) about herself. She then feels that whatever is neurotic should be discussed in psychotherapy, while what is normal can be pushed aside as nonsignificant. By his questions and remarks, the therapist attempts to teach the patient that in their meetings he wants to hear every aspect of herself, whether she feels it is pertinent or not.

When the therapist successfully communicates this nonjudgmental attitude, the patient can become accustomed to the idea in therapy that to discuss, study, and understand something in him is not synonymous with condemning it. Once an attitude of his is worked through in this manner, he is free to choose then whether he wants to change it or keep it.

The Therapist Learns

In the beginning stages of therapy, while the patient is getting used to the various educational conditions of the interview, the therapist is busy learning as much as he can about the patient. The therapist allows him to talk freely about whatever he is interested in telling. Once working clinical and dynamic diagnoses are established, the therapist listens for further data on those leading neurotic conflicts which he will eventually make the main precinct of interpretations. He tries to get a clearer picture of the patient's presenting difficulty in reference to past and present interpersonal relationships and in terms of compensating and decompensating ego functions.

Much of what the patient says at first may be a mystery in that you can't immediately see its relevance to his symptoms or problem. But this is quite natural and happens to veterans as well as to beginners in psychotherapy. "No man can hope to understand all that he daily beholds." This is because the patient never states the conflict directly or in so many words. Part or most of it is hidden from himself. It is only from the patient's verbalized allusions and approximations to his un- or preconscious conflicts that the therapist is able gradually to formulate their nature and extent.

In selecting the sector intended for therapy, the therapist pays particular attention to certain data, e.g., the situation coincident with the onset or exacerbation of symptoms, transference references, fantasies, dreams, and the patient's characteristic resistances. Each of these areas is a key source of information providing material enabling the therapist to understand and eventually interpret the underlying processes. Since we choose a sector of what the patient produces and let the rest go, the subsequent interpretations will be planned in the main to pivot around this sector.

Rather than having difficulty in clarifying the interpretable sector, the beginner may have more of a problem in restraining his eagerness to interpret something the moment it is glimpsed. That something is seen by the therapist does not automatically render it fit for interpretation. As is shown by the clinical examples thus far mentioned, the therapist's remarks in the beginning stage consist of interpositions (questions, explanations, advisory suggestions, etc.) rather than interpretations (confrontations with what is being warded off).

Also one must guard against a tendency to squeeze the patient into a prematurely formulated theory or even sometimes to fit the patient into a theory one is currently reading about. The chief activities of the therapist in these early interviews are listening and occasionally questioning. Even the questions should be limited and not too numerous, so as to avoid muzzling the patient's spontaneous remarks. It is true that at times the therapist must give reassurances or perhaps point out something to the knowledge-hungry patient just to keep the therapy going for a few more interviews until more extensive interpretations can be made.

Finally, beside learning of the patient's life experiences and how they bear on his central conflicts, the therapist soon gains an acquaintance with *how* the patient describes things. His typical words and phrases used in communication give you an opportunity to develop a common, quasi-private language together. This shared idiom allows the therapist short-cuts in phrasing interpositions and interpretations by knowing what certain words and images convey to the patient.

Drugs and Relatives

Among the manifold problems requiring direct action on the part of the therapist, two situations occurring most often in the beginning of therapy merit attention. They are (a) when the patient requests a prescription for drugs and (b) when friends or relatives wish to consult the therapist.

Drugs.—Some patients entering therapy are already taking drugs, usually benzedrine or barbiturates, prescribed by another physician. Others ask for drugs from the therapist to relieve their symptoms. In supportive or covering psychotherapy, small doses of drugs may be an expedient aid to the rallying of old healing defenses (repression, isolation, etc.). But in a mainly uncovering therapy, drugs must be avoided unless some pressing emergency arises. The therapist can frankly indicate his stand to the patient.

LOSING sleep because he fears that when he lies down at night his throat might close off, a young patient with an anxiety neurosis has been taking nembutal occasionally. In the third interview he asks for a prescription.

PT.: Dr. T. gave me a prescription some time ago for sleeping pills, and now I've run out. I was wondering if you could give me another one.
THER.: How often do you take them?
PT.: Once or twice a week my fear will keep me awake for a' couple of hours, then I take one. It usually puts me right to sleep.
THER.: I'd rather that you try to get along without them.
PT.: Why is that?
THER. (definitively): We agree that your anxiety is something purely psychological. For a psychological illness the best treatment is purely psychological. These sedatives are only

a temporary crutch. Let's try it without them. If it doesn't work out we can always reconsider it.

Most patients taking drugs before therapy, except the true addicts, of course, can soon abandon them. Sometimes at the beginning of psychotherapy when the patient genuinely suffers from prolonged painful tension or severe insomnia, sedatives can be prescribed as an emergency measure. In the course of therapy drugs should not be given unless the therapist feels there is a real crisis at hand.

Relatives.—Friends or relatives of the patient can be a mixed blessing. In supportive work they may be vital factors in manipulating situational improvements. At other times they may consciously or unconsciously undermine therapeutic efforts.

No friend or relative of the patient in therapy should be seen by the therapist without the spoken knowledge and permission of the patient. If the patient objects, then the relative cannot be allowed a visit. It the patient agrees, then the relative should understand that his conversation with the therapist will be reported to the patient. These requirements often are sufficient to discourage potential meddlers. The following telephone conversation between relative and therapist is typical:

THE pleasant voice at the other end of the line belongs to the mother of a thirty-two-year-old man who has often bitterly complained to the therapist that his mother always tries to interfere in his affairs.

MOTHER: Doctor, I'd like to have a talk with you about Peter.
THER.: Yes, I could see you. But I would have to talk it over with him first to see how he feels about it.
MOTHER: But that's just what I don't want. If he knew about it, he'd have a fit. Couldn't I see you without him knowing about it?

THER: I'm sorry, no.

MOTHER (*voice now not so pleasant*): Well, I must say that's a
   rather high-handed attitude. After all, I'm his mother and
   not a stranger.

THER.: I'll discuss your call with Peter next time.

MOTHER: I know he won't agree, so let's forget it.

Even such phone conversations should be mentioned to
the patient. If a relationship of trust is to develop between
patient and therapist, the therapist must be prepared to
demonstrate that he is straightforward and honest in his
attempts to be of help to the patient.

An Illustrative Series of Interviews

A condensed account of the first four interviews of uncovering psychotherapy in a clinical case is now presented
to illustrate some of the principles outlined in this chapter.
The therapist's thoughts and observations accompany the
patient's remarks.

First Interview.

THE patient is a twenty-six-year-old businessman referred to the
psychotherapist because of anxiety symptoms. After the introduction and seating, the therapist begins:

THER.: Well, where shall we start?

PT. (*smiling but uneasy*): I'm not sure. Perhaps I should go
   back a little to when I got these stomach things. They came
   on about six months ago. I was working hard and had a lot
   on my mind. I began to notice sort of a clutching sensation
   in the pit of my stomach, like something had suddenly
   clamped tight. I went to the doctor and he advised X-rays to
   look for an ulcer. The X-rays . . . .

THE therapist allows him to tell his story. He begins with his
physical symptoms, describing at some length the medical processes involved in establishing that he has no ulcer or other physi-

cal disease. In appearance he is an alert, friendly young man in a good humor.

Pt.: . . . so then I realized it was all emotional. I half suspected it at the time because I was under a lot of pressure. (*Stops.*)

Ther.: From what?

Pt. (*face serious*): The job, for one thing. There's a lot of politics in that office. I'm trying all the time to keep the different factions happy. And one or the other side is usually mad at me, thinking that I'm favoring the other one.

Ther.: What do you do?

This is a general information question. The therapist postpones for the time being further investigation of the "pressure" the patient connects with his symptoms. For a while the patient's job is discussed. He is able, successful, and ambitious. He had a college education before he entered the firm he now works for and has enjoyed several promotions. All this the patient reveals freely, at times laughing and joking. Now he is a little more at ease in the interview, perhaps because the topic is one he likes to relate and the therapist seems interested. But looking for data more directly pertinent to the symptoms, the therapist switches back to the earlier point.

Ther.: You said you were under a lot of pressure when this began. Anything else besides your job?

Pt. (*immediately loses some of his gaiety*): Yeah. I think even more important than the job is the trouble at home. My wife and I have our little spats like any other couple. But it's more than that. We can't seem to get together on our sex life.

He then tells of his marriage three years ago. His wife is from a similar New England background but seems never to have overcome many of her fears and dislikes of intercourse. He feels he is of an affectionate nature and likes to have intercourse every day while her desire emerges only two or three times a month. It is when they argue over this matter—she accusing him of being oversexed and he accusing her of being frigid—that his stomach spasms and anxiety develop. During this account he looks angry and bitter. The therapist notes to himself for future reference

(a) the wife as the important object relationship, (b) the high frequency of the patient's desired sexual activity, and (c) the stomach as the organ most affected by his anxiety.

PT.: . . . and I'm convinced that unless we can work this out I'm going to leave. Maybe she should see a psychiatrist, too. I don't want to leave her, she's everything I want in a wife outside of this sexual thing. She's attractive, intelligent, on the ball. But we can't go on this way.

THER.: How did you meet her?

Now gathering historical information on this important interpersonal relationship. The therapist does not subject the patient to the "routine psychiatric history" process but takes each item as it arises and, if it appears significant, explores it briefly.

In telling of meeting his wife and the courtship, an interesting fact comes to light. Before he was married, he was a heavy drinker but only after working hours. Each night he would go out with friends to bars or night clubs and get drunk. He told his girl friend, later his wife, that he didn't want to get married just yet. But one night he passed out and on coming to found himself in jail charged with disorderly conduct. This scared him so much that he decided he must settle down with a more stable life and hence the next day he proposed marriage.

THER.: And was the sexual problem present from the first?

PT.: Oh, yes. Even before we were married we tried intercourse and I knew she had trouble enjoying it. But I thought she would get over it as time went by.

THUS it becomes evident that there is more to this situation than sexual incompatability. He married her, knowing fully about her frigidity, in order to solve some internal problem till then being warded off through alcohol.

By this time the end of the hour is drawing near and the therapist wishes to arrange further appointments.

THER.: Well, our time is about up. You understand I can't say very much about all this right now.

PT.: Do you think you can help me?

THER.: (*smiling*): I'll certainly try. But let's work along a little further to see how it goes. Could you come again Friday at this time?

PT.: Okay. Fine.

THER.: For the time being let's talk Tuesday and Friday at this time. If these times don't work out we can consider some other arrangement.

THE tentative clinical diagnosis is anxiety neurosis. There is no evidence of a physical disease or psychosis. As yet the information is too meager to clearly formulate a dynamic diagnosis, but the therapist already feels that the patient is suitable for psychotherapy because of his age, intelligence, reliability, interest, and psychological awareness of a connection between his symptoms and a life problem which he is able to verbalize.

Second Interview.

HE arrives early. The interview begins with the therapist waiting for him to speak.

PT.: Where shall I start, doctor?

THER.: Anywhere you like. (*Immediately leaving the patient to choose the topic.*)

PT.: I like this idea of talking over my problems. During the time I was telling you about, when I drank so much, I sometimes thought to myself, "You're all screwed up, you should see a psychiatrist." But I guess I didn't have the courage.

THER.: Now that you can look back on it, why do you think you did drink so much during that period?

PT.: You've got me there. One thing it does is relax my stomach.

THER. (*interrupting*): You mean your stomach spasmed at that time?

PT.: Off and on. I guess it's come and gone for years. Nowadays it's the worst it's ever been. In those days I didn't know why it was acting up. Didn't even know my wife then. H'mph (*surprised*). That's odd, never thought of it until just now. I had stomach trouble six or seven years ago when I was going to school. That's when my drinking began. I started going out with the boys for a beer, and soon we were getting blotto every week end.

HERE the therapist finds partial confirmation of his conclusion in the first interview that something was upsetting the patient before his marriage.

PT.: I enjoyed those times. It was the feeling of freedom, or doing whatever the hell I wanted to. For the first time in my life nobody was checking up on me. That's what I couldn't stand about home, a feeling of restriction.

THER.: Your parents kept close watch over you?

PT.: (*vehemently*): And how! When I was seventeen they still treated me like a child. I couldn't go out at night unless I told them where I was going, who I'd be with, etc. My mother especially, my father didn't care too much.

WITH the introduction of home and parents into the discussion the therapist then asks a few questions about them. Summarizing, both his parents were teachers and he was their only child. Of moderate income and social position, the family lived comfortably and quietly in a large city As he talks now, he emphasizes his father's fanatical pursuit of physical culture and his mother's peevishness. The therapist returns to the patient's drinking, seeking further information for a dynamic diagnosis. He restates the patient's own judgment.

THER.: So one thing in the drinking was feeling independent?

PT.: And the comradeship. It was fun. We'd have big bull sessions and talk for hours.

THER.: What do you connect your stomach troubles with at that time?

PT.: Another thing that relaxed me at times were day-dreams. One especially about meeting a woman somewhere and getting together with her.

HE avoids the question as if he hadn't heard it. Why this reluctance? His anxiety related to being with other men? His mind jumped to having an affair with a woman. His heterosexuality exaggerated as a defense? The therapist lets this evasion go by without comment. Now comes a fantasy, always a fruitful source of revelation.

PT.: . . . though actually I don't know if I'd carry it out. I've had chances to shack up with several women but somehow it never works out.

THER.: What sort of woman do you think about?

PT. (*laughs*): Well, that's an interesting thing. It's always a large, big-breasted woman-of-the-world type—a little older and more experienced. She would be my mistress, though, not a wife. She's just the opposite of the way my wife is. She'd be sort of motherly. My wife isn't at all affectionate that way. She's a cold fish. When I come back from a business trip, she says hello as if I'd just gone down to the corner to mail a letter. That's why I like to get away at times. Escape both the office and home. And I enjoy traveling. It gives me a feeling of importance to travel on some important job. I know things center around me, that I can do a good job.

THE fantasy and his associations to it show in terms of object relationships, his wish for a mother, and the frustration of this wish in his relationship to his wife. In structural terms, his ego fails to successfully deal with passive-receptive wishes, though the sublimations and compensations found in his work do bring gratification. At this point then, the dynamic diagnosis would formulate his chief neurotic conflicts as revolving around dependency on wife and mother and possibly fears of this passive orientation in relation to men. Since the symptomatic process is only of a few years' duration and the patient is young, pliable, and "psychologically minded," it is worth while to attempt an uncovering therapy which will endeavor to make conscious some of these unconscious factors.

Since the time is up:

THER.: Okay. Let's stop there for today.

PT. (*arising*): Should I write down things during the day for you to read? Maybe you could find out more about me than by just what I say here.

THER.: No, that isn't necessary. See you Tuesday.

Third Interview.

As the patient enters he takes off his suit coat and hangs it on the back of his chair. This is an important observation for the therapist, since he himself does not wear a suit coat while working. The patient's first remarks also constitute a transference reference.

Pt.: Is this psychotherapy I'm getting?
Ther.: Yes. What interests you in that regard?
Pt.: The other night I was talking with my friends about the difference between psychotherapy and psychoanalysis, and none of us could get it very clearly. I know in psychoanalysis the patient lies down. And I see you have a couch. Do you want me to lie down?
Ther.: No. We can work along this way for the time being.

Perhaps he wants to lie down (be in a more submissive position) and in preparation for it took off his coat. The therapist awaits the common question as to whether he is an analyst or not.

Pt.: Do you use psychoanalysis in this clinic?
Ther.: No, but we call it psychoanalytic psychotherapy. That is, we look at things from a more or less psychoanalytic viewpoint.

In answer to the testing-out questions, the therapist gives simple explanations, by-passing the underlying significance of the questions. The patient returns to describing his symptoms.

Pt.: My stomach is just about the same. The other day on the bus I really noticed it. Like a vise gripping me in the pit of the stomach. I was sweating a little and felt uneasy. Nothing I could think of on the bus upset me. It comes on like that sometimes, out of the blue. What do you think it could be?
Ther. (shrugging): Oh, I don't know. It sounds like a little spell of anxiety that comes and goes.
Pt.: I know I feel anxious during it. Sometimes I can feel my heart beating, too. What scared me at first was the idea that I had something really wrong. Like an ulcer or maybe appendicitis.

At this stage in the interview the patient seems preoccupied only with his bodily symptoms and in elaborating on them. He does not continue into his past or present life experiences. That plus the glimmering of transference phenomena indicated at the start of the hour signify to the therapist the presence of a force beginning to impede the desired course of therapy (cf. page 95 for further discussion of resistances). Again this is not pointed out to the patient. The therapist waits until a key word or phrase appears in the patient's comments which will serve as a springboard to a topic away from symptom-rumination.

PT.: . . . but when I told my wife that I had an ulcer, she just laughed. I looked up ulcers in a medical book and found that there was some comparison.

THER.: Your wife didn't take you seriously?

PT.: She never thinks I'm sick. If I tell her I have the flu or don't feel well, she passes it off as if I were just complaining. But when she's sick you'd think she was dying. She's always getting sick with this or that.

Now the patient's attention is away from his symptoms and on his major interpersonal relationship. The therapist holds him there by asking several more questions about his wife, helping the patient to unfold more and more of his feelings about her. Soon the intercourse problem enters the discussion and something of the patient's past sexual life is learned. In late adolescence he began sex play with a girl his own age. For several months they met three and four times a day for kissing, petting, and mutual masturbation. Fearing pregnancy, she would not permit intercourse. This high frequency of sexual activity gratified him immensely. He had several ejaculations a day and never seemed to tire of it. During the sex play his accompanying fantasies were of intercourse, mostly with the girl but often with the worldly woman of his day-dreams. Wondering about a temporal sequence, the therapist asks:

THER.: And is this when your heavy drinking began?

PT.: No, the drinking came later. I fooled around with this girl when I was eighteen. The drinking started when I was nineteen or twenty.

THE therapist has in mind that the hypersexuality, being not truly on a genital level of development, not only gratified some impulses but also served defensive purposes similarly to the heavy drinking.

Fourth Interview.

TODAY he looks a little more uneasy than last time. He immediately lights a cigarette.

PT.: Tell me, what did you think of the Kinsey report?

THER.: Or of more interest, what did you think of it?

PT.: It was a comfort in one way. Especially the figures on masturbation. And the part about homosexuality. I never realized how many men had such an experience. I must admit I've worried whether I've had any homosexual trends. (*Voice shaky.*)

THER. (*matter-of-factly*): Why?

PT.: I've read about men who become homosexual when there are no women around—like in prison. I've thought that, since my wife wants so little sex, maybe it would drive me in that direction. I knew a guy once who was homosexual. He was a classmate in college, brilliant guy. He was very open about it. We used to talk about it a lot. He claimed homosexuals were a persecuted minority and someone should go to work on this prejudice like the work being done on anti-Semitism. That's something I have fights over with my father. He's a real reactionary. Why, he even thinks that labor leaders should be shot.

HAVING for a moment faced his anxiety about homosexuality, he now skitters away to a less tension-evoking topic, though the therapist notes that it concerns his difference from his father. It is too early in therapy, with the transference undeveloped and the patient too scared by the subject's significance, to force prolonged exploration of homosexual pathways. The topic will crop up again directly or indirectly in subsequent interviews.

Continuing to relate his father's social and political views, he soon approaches his struggles in breaking away from what he felt was a severe parental constriction and domination. The clash of children and parents is a subject the therapist listens to very attentively, knowing that this is stuff out of which transferences are fashioned, especially in the case of male patients.

Pt.: When I visit them nowadays, I still feel some of that old op-
pression. Like at the table my father will say, "All those guys
in Washington are a bunch of crooks. Roosevelt was a
crook." It burns me up, but I don't say anything. What
good would it do?

Ther.: Maybe he's trying to get a rise out of you.

Pt.: No. He's just making flat statements as if he were telling
us this is the way it is and there's no question about it.

And so it goes. Let us now turn to the middle course of
psychotherapy, characterized by the actual work of interpretation designed to modify neurotic conflicts.

Chapter 7

THE MIDDLE COURSE OF THERAPY

For discussion purposes we can designate the middle period of therapy as ranging from the first interpretations on to the very end of therapy. With the first interpretations the bulk of therapeutic work begins. In theory this work will consist of freeing the ego of a symptom-producing neurotic conflict. In practice, the chief technical tools for the task are the therapist's remarks, which fall into two groups, (a) interpositions and (b) interpretations. The preceding chapter has already considered the rationale and use of interpositions. They continue through the course of therapy. Interpretations, more characteristic of the middle period, will now be examined and discussed.

Interpretations

An *interpretation* is a statement, phrased in one of various ways, which the therapist makes in reference to something the patient has said or done. The therapeutic intent of the statement is to confront the patient with something in himself which he has warded off and of which he is partially or totally unaware. Thus the unconscious is made conscious.

First, I propose to discuss the *what* of interpretation, later the *how* and *where*.

The most common interpretations a psychotherapist uses can be divided into three categories: (a) clarification interpretations, (b) comparison interpretations, and (c) wish-defense interpretations.

Clarification Interpretations.—These are statements by the therapist made to crystallize the patient's thoughts and feelings around a particular subject, to focus his attention on something requiring further investigation and interpretation, to sort out a theme from apparently diversified material, or to summarize the understanding thus far achieved. They may take the form of questions, mild imperatives, or simplified restatements.   Here are clinical examples.

1. DURING the middle of therapy for a marital problem, a young woman describes a brief period of new symptoms resembling a physical illness—malaise, fatigue, loss of appetite. In preceding interviews various aspects of her relationship to her husband had been discussed. They were both students in the same field, competing for academic success. She was the more successful and dominant of the two. Only recently has she become more aware that the husband is also in one sense her child whom she protects, regulates, and manages.
The symptoms she now describes developed during a trip which she decided to take without her husband in spite of his pleas to go along. On the trip her determination to be alone wilted and she began to "feel like a heel" for leaving her husband behind. She begins to elaborate on her activities during the short vacation, but the therapist at this point wishes to restate the connection between symptoms and life experience in a clarifying and focusing way.

THER.: So you feel guilty about frustrating your husband's wishes?
PT.: That's right. After all, he wouldn't have been too much trouble. And he looked so hurt.
THER.: Perhaps your tiredness was connected with this.

2. IN each of the first few interviews, a young man has spent most of the time describing the events of several love-affairs. None of them worked out very satisfactorily. Sooner or later there would be an argument or falling-out.

The therapist has been struck by a characteristic of these affairs as yet unmentioned by the patient, namely that, in all but one instance, he was at ease within himself when the affair was platonic, while, when intercourse took place, an inner turmoil developed with insomnia, restlessness, etc. Thus far the therapist's remarks have been confined to interpositions. Now he wishes to point out this theme and send the patient's further thoughts along these lines.

THER.: It seems in these affairs you've described, that when intercourse began is when you began to get upset.
PT.: Yes, I've thought of that, too.   Don't know what it is exactly.
THER.: And when you began to get upset, then the arguments would start?

3. SEVERAL interviews ago the discussion touched on this soldier's fear of tough or aggressive men. At that time the therapist had been able to show the patient one aspect of this fear, i.e., that he might do something which would provoke an attack on himself. The patient agreed there was something to this. However, in subsequent interviews he did not continue with this topic, preferring to give attention to other matters.

Now in this interview the patient again brings up his fear of belligerent men, citing an example which recently happened. He again expresses puzzlement over why such a thing should bother him.

PT.: I can't understand it. There's no reason for it. I've never been in a fight. I get along pretty well with everybody. It's all very confusing.
THER.: Last time when we talked about this, it looked as if you were afraid you might provoke some attack or fight.

THE therapist restates a previous interpretation, clarifying a starting point for the patient to think about.

Comparison Interpretations.—In these statements the therapist places two (or more) sets of events, thoughts or feelings side by side for comparison. They may parallel one

another or show contrast.   They may be concurrent or separated in time.   Common typical subjects compared are past
with present behavior, fantasy with reality, the patient's self
with others, childhood with adulthood and attitude toward
parent with attitude toward friend, spouse, or therapist.
Comparisons may be used to emphasize patterns of repeti-
tive similarities or to indicate recurring contradictions. They
may be phrased in any form, the most frequent being the
everyday ways of matching things.

1.   OUTSTANDING in this man's life has been his rebellion against
his father as a person and as a representative of certain social
values.   In previous interviews he has given the therapist an extensive roster of traits that he finds repellent in his father.

Today, having not referred to the father for a few interviews,
he reports how he enjoys entering a bar where he is well known.
The bartenders, the waitresses, and the regular patrons give him
the glad hello, and when he moves from table to table chatting
and joking he gets the pleasant feeling of being a "big shot."
The therapist recalls that one of the patient's complaints is that
his father often acts the part of a "big shot" among his friends.
The therapist then compares the patient's behavior with that of
his father.

THER.: In a way, isn't that like what your father does?
PT.: How so?
THER.: You mentioned once that it griped you how your father
    acted like a big shot. Now you say that you sometimes enjoy
    being like a big shot.

2.   NEAR the beginning of the hour a woman of Lutheran background recounted a painful childhood memory in which at age
four she was severely shamed by her mother for showing her underwear to assembled house guests.   From this she went on to
other aspects of her early training.   Soon her mind traveled to
present-day happenings, including references to an extramarital
affair.   Before, when she has tried to talk about this affair, she
implied that there was something about her sexually which her
husband cannot satisfy but which her lover can.   It has never

been clear what this is, because the patient becomes embarrassed and immediately shies away from the topic.

She again approaches the subject but blushingly hesitates and looks vexed. The therapist makes a comparison.

PT.: I don't know why it is. I never can seem to bring myself to say it, though I know I should talk about it. Maybe because it's such a private thing.

THER.: Or it's like showing your underwear to strangers.

3. ONCE a patient arrived late for her interview. She explained that she didn't own a watch. She kept track of the time at home by the radio and outside the home by public clocks or by asking people she happened to be with.

Many interviews later, the patient is describing some of her personality characteristics. She says she is a very efficient, businesslike person who takes problems as they arise and solves them as soon as possible. In particular it bothers her to be late for anything, and she makes strenuous efforts to be on time. The therapist compares these two sets of facts to point out their contrast.

THER.: But you said you don't have a watch.

PT.: That's right. I haven't had one for several years.

THER.: That's somewhat contradictory, isn't it? On the one hand you say you like to be punctual. On the other hand you don't have a watch, so you're never quite sure what time it is.

Wish-Defense Interpretations.—Into this category fall those statements of the therapist which directly point to the wish-defense components of a neurotic conflict. Though we speak theoretically of wish and defense as separate elements in a conflict, it is difficult in practice to observe or deal with one or the other in a pure form. What we see empirically and manipulate are ego mechanisms, alloys of both wishes and defenses. One isolated component cannot be handled without implicitly or explicitly involving the other.

However, it must be strongly emphasized to the beginning therapist that we try, as far as possible, to interpret *first* the defense element of the wish-defense system, as is illustrated in the following examples.

1. THERAPY with an overtly homosexual man in his early twenties, suffering from acute anxiety, had progressed to the point where it became clear that his greatest fear was of being approached by a certain type of man. The latter was a tall, muscular, and strong brute, easily enraged by any opposition to his wishes.

While in therapy the patient was picked up by such a man, who became drunk and powerless. As long as he could control his helpless companion and determine their sexual practices, the patient felt no fear. But as the man sobered up and suddenly insisted that the patient lie down, he became panicky and fled.

In approaching the conflict around the patient's unconscious and warded-off wish to be treated like a woman by another man, the therapist avoids confronting him with this impulse. The interpretation first refers to the patient's anxiety and flight in terms of his defense of projection.

THER.: You get afraid of the strong man when it seems he can do something to you. What do you fear he wants to do?

2. THE husband of this patient complains that she is a constant nag and this trait is responsible for his drinking. However, she feels that what he calls nagging is really her motherly concern for his welfare. From evidence gathered in previous interviews, the therapist knows that behind her kind protectiveness lie sadistic impulses toward the husband. But interpretations around this subject are first made in reference to her defense, not her wish-impulse.

THER.: Do you feel you are *overly* protective toward him?
PT.: Maybe at times. Like if a rainstorm comes up during the day, I worry he might be caught in it. That's silly because there's no reason to think he couldn't be in a dry place.
THER.: And he gets annoyed when you fuss over him?
PT.: He says it's too much. I mother him, but I don't think it's that bad.
THER.: But why do you think your concern is so exaggerated? It's as if you were afraid he's always in danger of something.

How to Present Interpretations.—Clarification, comparison and wish-defense interpretations comprise the *what* of the usual confrontations made by the therapist. Next to be considered is *how* such statements are presented to the patient.

In brief, the interpretations of the therapist take all the grammatical forms common to everyday nontechnical language. Technical psychiatric words and phrases (masochism, Oedipus, etc.) are purely shorthand terms of convenience for scientific discussions and have no place in statements to the patient. Similar content in interpretations can be expressed in several ways, and in this sense the therapist's horn should have more than one note. For instance, the ideational content of an interpretation might refer to a patient's unrecognized fear of physical violence. This idea could be stated by the therapist as:

A question: "Do you think you could be afraid of violence?"

A suggestion: "Perhaps you really fear violence" [or] "That sounds like you fear violence."

A tentative assertion: "My feeling is that you are afraid of violence."

A pronouncement: "Violence frightens you!"

Of course, besides the verbal form, the therapist's accompanying tone of voice, gestures and facial expression (if *vis-à-vis*) carry an impact. This is an area uncharted by rules. One principle of help to the beginner is that he should interpret by and large in the form of questions or suggestions, avoiding the brandishment of his ideas with an air of finality. If the therapist offers, in words and tone, his comments as provisional statements, his method will circumvent unnecessarily induced resistances which arise from trying to force the patient to accept a gospel. H. Sullivan felt that really useful interpretations were "alternative hypotheses."

A second aspect of the manner in which interpretations are presented concerns the degrees of exactness and directness used in confrontation. Since the therapist does not immediately and incisively point to the fended-off area but prefers to lead the patient to it step by step, his interpretations vary in specificity from the first approach to the eventual disclosure. Thus the early statements on some topic are more generalized and open-ended, allowing them to be taken up by the patient in ways of his choice. N. Reider feels that the best initial interpretations are simply restatements of the problem in somewhat more dynamic terms. An illustrative example follows:

UNFORTUNATELY the major personality characteristic of a young clerk was to alienate those who wanted to be friends with him. In fact, he provokes rejection only from people who are in a position to help him.

As therapy progressed, he naturally began to involve the therapist in his standard interpersonal plot. From the transference sample and from other illustrations, the therapist could see that the patient fears liking someone since, due to certain childhood experiences, it is tantamount to causing their death. Thus in approaching this conflict the initial interpretations are presented, necessarily at different times, as:

Do you feel that he rejected you for no good reason?
Perhaps you had something to do with the break-up.
That looks like you might have provoked him a little.
We should have to wonder why you partly engineer these rejections.

As these interpretations are gradually accepted and assimilated by the patient, the therapist later becomes more direct and finally specific. It is to be understood that all these interpretations ranged over the course of many interviews and were woven into other remarks on other topics:

Do you think maybe you are afraid of something the more you get to know someone?

Are you afraid of getting too close to him?
Perhaps what bothers you is liking the person.
If you like him, something will happen to him.
What you fear is that what happened to your brother might
   happen to him.

A final point to be considered in the *how* of interpretation concerns the frequency and extent of the therapist's remarks. It is best to interpret sparsely and succinctly rather than to respond capriciously and copiously to everything interpretable. A therapist should talk less than his patient. Just as with too many interpositions, if the patient is sprayed with interpretations, he soon feels befuddled and swamped by things to think about. This can induce a chaotic therapeutic situation. Effective interpretations are concise, simply phrased, and few in number, begin as approximations on the periphery, and end as convergences on the center.

Timing.—Next comes the difficult subject of *when* an interpretation is given. Again, to state rules is as impossible as to speak generally about what players should do on the seventeenth move of chess games. At best we can only sketch a few elements characteristic of good interpretive timing.

As we saw in the use of interpositions (cf. page 42), the therapist takes note of the fluctuating tension-levels shown by the patient during an interview. An optimum level of anxiety is one sufficient to stir the patient to make the effort required in a psychotherapeutic interview, but not one of such a degree as to put his participating ego out of commission. Thus when anxiety (or some other affect) mounts to the extent of threatening the patient's ability to observe and report himself, the therapist steps in with an interposition or an interpretation to circumvent the interference. An apt metaphor of S. Bernfeld's compares the activity of a psychotherapist to the activity of a life-guard who for the most part sits and watches but who intervenes quickly when things go amiss.

Of greater importance in timing than the tension-state, which can be controlled solely with interpositions or "coasting" interpretations, is the learning state of the patient. That is, can he, with what he knows of himself at this point, grasp the interpretation and see its pertinent validity? This, of course, depends on the nature and function of his resistances (cf. page 99). Like pushing a playground swing at the height of its arc for optimum momentum, the best-timed interpretations are given when the patient, already close to it himself, requires only a nudge to help him see the hitherto unseen.

Dosage.—Closely associated with the problem of timing is that of dosage of interpretation. On page 89 it was mentioned that the patient's conflicts are approached only gradually over an extended period of time. How much the patient is shown each time is termed "dosage." Small doses (again the factor of resistances comes into play) are the most advantageous. A second principle involves the patient's self-esteem. An interpretation should be only of a dosage which spares the patient a severe loss of self-esteem or any other painful affect to which he is susceptible. Patients vary in their ability to tolerate affect tensions, and the therapist soon learns how slowly he must approach with confrontations and of what doses they can consist.

At times the patient may not agree with an interpretation. This does not necessarily mean that it is incorrect, dynamically or economically. One tries to interpret at the point of least resistance at the appropriate moment, but of course such theoretical precision is often technically impossible. If the patient does not accept an interpretation, the

therapist should beware of arguing with him to force conviction.   Strong opposition on the part of the patient is a signal
for a temporary and graceful retreat, as in the following example:

A SYMPTOM of an obsessive-compulsive woman in her twenties is
the uncomfortably frequent thought that something disastrous
might happen to her mother.   Because of this she is intensely
concerned with her mother's well-being, regularly phoning home
several times a day to see if all is well.

Already several weeks of therapy have gone by in which her
relationship to her mother has frequently been touched upon.
In this interview she describes an argument with her mother over
money in which she suddenly became very upset and anxious to
the point where she had to leave the room.

THER.: And how did you feel?
PT.: Sick of the whole thing.   It was only about fifteen cents, and
   why should there by such a fuss about so little?

Now the therapist attempts an interpretation in the form of a
question which, though probably accurate in content, comes too
close to the underlying conflict too fast and hence is resisted.

THER.: Did you feel some hostility toward your mother?
PT. (*indignantly recoiling*): Oh, of course not!   I love my mother
   very much.   How could you suggest such a thing?
THER. (*affably*): It occurred to me, but don't take everything I
   say as necessarily true.   I'm often wrong.   My comments are
   meant only as trial balloons to see what thoughts they bring
   to your mind.   In this case you feel that hostility was out of
   the question, that you have only friendly feelings toward your
   mother.
PT.: That's right.   We do have little squabbles at times, but they
   never amount to very much.
THER. (*moving on*): What other things do you squabble about?

Thus interpretations made tentatively or as questions have
the added value of skirting the possible full arousal of impor-

tant resistances. The therapist can look at all interpretations as having an evocative as well as confronting purpose. Though the patient may not agree, the nature and intensity of the kindled response provide further psychological data to be examined.

Assessing the Effect.—Psychotherapists, veterans as well as beginners, often wonder how to tell whether an interpretation is effective. Actually we never know exactly which remarks have produced a dynamic change in the patient's conflict. Similarly, at the moment when an individual interpretation is given, we may be unsure of its effect. Simple agreement or disagreement on the part of the patient is insufficient evidence. He may agree verbally to please you or avoid a feared argument, or he may disagree for a host of reasons, while his subsequent remarks show that part of him fully accepts the interpretation.

Correct interpretations often produce a feeling of surprise or startled illumination which the patient expresses in the form of a short laugh and eye-opening. Probably the most useful index of the effectiveness of an interpretation consists of the patient's subsequent productions in the interview. If he gives the interpretation room in his mind, freely thinks out loud about it, and brings corroborative evidence from the present or past, then both confronting and evocative purposes are being served. Even if the patient is skeptical of the interpretation's validity but continues to produce thoughts, whether in the indicated direction or not, an evocative purpose is at least served, though the actual confrontations may have misfired. This event is reminiscent of A. N. Whitehead's "the basic quality of any proposition is not that it be true but that it be interesting and exciting." The following example illustrates how an interpretation may be followed up:

A BEWILDERED college student comes to therapy for help in deciding whether to leave school or remain. The latter course is the wish of his parents, to whom he feels deeply indebted. However, he is not genuinely interested in college work and would prefer to study a craft. His indecisive vacillations have precipitated symptoms of anxiety and depression.

The day before this interview while he was at a party given by friends, one of his professors entered the room. The patient immediately became uneasy and developed his anxiety symptoms of flushing and sweating. The professor was a friend of his parents and also knew of his poor school performance.

THER.: What thoughts were going through your mind there?
PT.: Well, he knew all about me. Everybody else there thinks I'm doing fine. It was sort of a guilty feeling, too—embarrassed. I remember I used to feel that way as a child whenever my mother would come around when I was playing with my friends. I didn't want them to see her. That was when everybody called her crazy.
THER.: You were afraid the professor would expose you?

THE therapist wishes to focus on the dynamics of the patient's reaction at the party. However, the patient dismisses this line of thought and continues his interest in the childhood situation with his mother.

PT.: No, I don't think so. You know I never got over that feeling that I didn't want others to meet my mother. We never knew when she would make a scene, and when she'd start yelling I'd just want to get out of there fast. And I felt guilty as if I had done something bad rather than she.

SINCE the attempt to show the patient what he feared from the professor is unsuccessful for the moment, the therapist follows the axis of thought being evoked.

THER.: Did you feel guilty about something else in connection with your mother?
PT.: Quite possibly. I don't remember feeling guilty, but either I must have or should have because I was told many times

that my mother wasn't always like this. It was after she gave birth to me that she had the nervous breakdown.

THER.: So in a way it was implied that you were responsible for her crazy scenes.

PT.: Yes, it would be. And that would be one reason why I'd feel embarrassed and want to run.

Comparing the confronting and evocative aspects of interpretation to serial tugs on a folding telescope, we see that each effort uncovers a larger and hitherto unseen segment of the anticipated whole.

Resistances

What serves as defense for the patient in his neurosis is directly observed by the therapist in the therapeutic interview as resistance. A defense operating against the efforts of therapy is termed a resistance. The characteristic defenses that the patient repetitively uses in warding off wish-impulses will be mobilized to ward off therapy as a threatened interference with neurotic equilibria. For instance, a patient whose sexual conflict originated in masturbation might speak freely in the interviews of intercourse but omit references to auto-erotic activities. Here the defense of repression blots out from the therapeutic situation what it correspondingly blots out in the patient's mind. An ideational representative of an instinctual drive is barred from the patient's consciousness and from being verbalized to the therapist.

Interpositions and interpretations which lessen and remove resistances thus nullify defenses and in so doing change the balance of wish-defense conflicts. The first requirement of the therapist in dealing with resistances is the ability to detect them. Some degree of resistance is naturally always present with fluctuating levels of intensity. Levels which seriously block therapy must be recognized and lessened.

Each patient from the beginning shows what may be called his base line of resistances. These are defenses determined by the patient's psychological past. The long-range aim of therapy is to gradually overcome some of these initial obstacles, while the short-range aim is to modify whatever increases take place from the base line as therapy progresses, i.e., intercurrent resistances. The latter are defenses arising out of the transference situation.

The common forms of resistances observed in everyday practice are listed below.

Quantity of Speech.—Each patient has his own pace in speaking, and once the therapist becomes familiar with it, variations are easily noticed. The patient may begin to pause more often and for longer intervals. He often says that his mind is blank or that he cannot think of subjects to discuss. He may become silent, restless and uneasy.

At the other extreme is constant overtalkativeness. Or a patient, previously of modest output, may suddenly become very loquacious. He states that he has so many thoughts he doesn't know which to select, and he hops from topic to topic in a rambling and verbose manner.

Quality of Speech.—Although the patient may talk freely enough at his usual pace, the subjects of his interest often announce the presence of resistances. He may circle endlessly around his symptoms, reviewing in detail the same material over and over. Or he may stick to one area of his life without broadening out into other related areas.

Instead of discussing the problems which brought him to therapy, he may spend his time speaking only of the therapist, seemingly having lost interest in anything else. Much of the interview may consist of the patient's intellectualizing in general or in a common form, psychologizing by testing out now one psychological theory and now another on himself. He may launch his detached views on the sterling or doubtful value of a psychological school and attempt to involve the therapist in these evaluations. Knowing that the therapist is a physician, the patient may speak only of medical matters and repeatedly request medical advice. Knowing also that psychotherapists are interested in hearing of sexual attitudes and activities, the patient may promptly and unhesitantly give a detailed and chronological account of his sexual life. Or he may offer a series of long and complex dreams for interpretations.

Frank omissions and censorships appear. The patient will mention that he saw someone who said something, but he cannot give the name or the content because that would be passing on gossip. He may omit mention of a feeling or a detail of an event which the therapist knows from the logic of emotions and everyday experience must have occurred.

L. Kubie summarizes the form-content aspects of the patient's speech eloquently: "From moment to moment the patient struggles with impulses to hold back or not to talk at all, or to rearrange his words into pleasanter and more acceptable forms; that is, into forms which are more flattering to his self-esteem and to the impression which he wants to make on the therapist."

External Interferences.—All sorts of hindrances to the occurrence, duration, and consistent repetition of the therapeutic interview may arise. The patient may repeatedly come late, forget the hour entirely, or cancel the appointment at the last minute for realistically insufficient reasons. He may arrange so many other activities in his life in such a way that few interviews take place and these are separated by long periods of time. Or frequent changes of the appointment hour are requested perhaps along with abbreviations in the length. Minor illnesses become excuses to avoid interviews.

Often slight improvement of the patient's neurosis may offer him reasons to interrupt or discontinue therapy.

Modifying Resistances.—With the recognition of the patient's base line and intercurrent resistances, the therapist's attempts to modify defenses begin. The next step in the therapist's mind consists of speculation about what is being resisted or defended against and why. The intercurrent resistances, stemming from transference and temporarily blocking the uncovering process, are the source of greatest immediate concern. If the therapist can understand their content and motivation, he can, of course, plan attempts to circumvent them, as in the following example:

For the past five or six years, a young man has suffered symptoms of depression and indecision. In the very first interview he mentioned also that he had been sexually impotent. However, in subsequent interviews there was absolutely nothing said about sexual matters for many weeks.

In the beginning stages of therapy the therapist learned of a typical pattern shown by the patient. Interviews took place on Friday and on the following Monday. Each interview began with the details of his everyday activities during the time between interviews. After about half the interview time was spent on these daily accounts, he would move on to discuss relationships and feelings. His interview base line is to speak rather easily and continuously with few pauses though some restlessness.

This hour is a Monday. Immediately a change in the patient's verbal and nonverbal behavior is noticeable. The interview begins with a prolonged silence. The patient frequently sighs, puts out a half-smoked cigarette to light another one, and shifts his position many times. Finally he begins by talking about an event of last week which he had discussed in the previous Friday hour. Long pauses develop with expressions such as "Let's see now" and "I should think of something."

Noting the omission of the usual week-end account and the other obvious signs of resistance, the therapist wonders what is being held back and why. Possibly the *what* occurred during the week-end and the *why* is anxiety over its specific nature. Recalling the long-range suppression of sexual data though a sexual problem is known to exist, the therapist's guess is that something sexual took place during the week-end which the patient is afraid to bring up because of his fear of the therapist's reaction.

THER.: What did you do over the week-end?
PT.: I knew I'd have to get to it sooner or later, so I might as well now. Saturday night I got drunk, dead drunk. I went with some of my friends to a whore-house. . . .

IN this case a simple question spoken in a matter-of-fact way was sufficient to overcome, without any interpretation, an interfering intercurrent resistance.

To understand the motive for a particular resistance, we have only to apply our understanding of the motive for defenses in general. Ego defenses originate and develop to discharge and bind tension. Tension is experienced as an unpleasant affect, largely anxiety (or its derivatives, guilt, shame, disgust) or rage. Since defense = resistance, the motive for a resistance is also an unpleasant affect which threatens to be evoked in the therapeutic process. The task of the therapist is then to formulate the answer to: "What is the patient afraid (or ashamed, etc.) of verbalizing?"

The content being fended off is deduced or guessed from one's over-all knowledge of the patient and the configuration of therapy at the moment of resistance. Many times, though he understands that the patient fears something and is avoiding it, the therapist is unable to grasp what the subject is. However, as will be shown (page 101), this does not necessarily prevent the removal of a resistance.

When timing and dosage of interpretations were mentioned (cf. page 90 f.), it was stated that the factor of resistances came into play. Now an additional principle governing interpretation can be presented, namely interpretations should be made at the point of least resistance. This implies that first interpretations are not made in reference to the chief symptoms, since we know that major defenses (resistances) operate in this area. A frontal attack on a strong defensive point is useless. Thus dealing with intercurrent resistances to begin with is more effective than tackling base-line resistances. By removing lesser obstacles at first, larger fragments of defense can be approached and meeting the full force of resistances at any one time can be avoided.

Long-term (base-line) and short-term (intercurrent) resistances are attenuated in part by (a) the general permissive atmosphere of therapy with the therapist's calm, nonscolding attitude, but mainly by (b) the therapist's interpositions and interpretations. Just as not every observable pattern or conflict is interpreted to the patient, so not every recognized resistance is directly discussed. In fact, in psychotherapy the majority of resistances are by-passed with no attempt to focus the patient's attention on them. Those of sufficient dimension to seriously hinder the uncovering process must be interpreted. In a covering or supportive psychotherapy almost all resistances are left in the patient's keeping.

Interpositions alone are often sufficient to overcome an intercurrent resistance. Here is an example in which a reassuring explanation is used:

SINCERELY attempting to say what comes to his mind, a man of religious background finds himself in an uncomfortable position because he is having repeated homosexual fantasies in which he wonders what other men's naked genitals look like. Besides being ashamed of such thoughts, he is frightened by them because they might mean he must become overtly homosexual to be happy. In therapy he has great difficulty in elaborating on these fantasies, merely saying from time to time that he has them. The therapist attempts to modify the patient's anxiety in order to learn more about the nature of the fantasies.

Pt.: I know I don't like to talk about it. I writhe inside. Mainly I'm scared about what they mean. Maybe I'm homosexual. As soon as I think that, I stop them and try to think about something else.

Ther.: Fantasies like that don't necessarily mean you're homosexual. They're just thoughts like any other thoughts. And, as you know, most thoughts are never acted upon.

Pt.: That's comforting to know.

Ther.: And what do you think your fantasies really wonder about these genitals?

The patient was better able to go into more valuable details once the anxiety motivating his resistance had been somewhat relieved by the therapist's interposition.

In the following example the therapist confronts the patient with one of his interview traits. This interpretation, in the form of a question, attempts to show the patient a defense he uses in the hope that through understanding it he can begin to abandon it. Noteworthy is the therapist's ignorance of the content or the motive for the base-line resistance.

Before or after most of his remarks, a young scholar would make interpretations of them based on his reading knowledge of psychology. From the first interview this has been an outstanding characteristic. As yet he has not been able to approach any of his life problems, preferring to intellectualize at length. The therapist is not at all certain why this resistance operates or what it is directed against, but he wishes to lessen its interference with the uncovering therapy. Hence he begins by pointing the resistance out to the patient in order to initiate its resolution.

Ther.: Have you noticed that you tend to interpret everything you say?

Pt.: Yes, I know. It's as if I wanted to get my interpretations in first before you do.

Now it appears that his defense of theorizing is connected with his thoughts about the therapist. In a sense he feels he too is an interpreter, a rival therapist.

THER.: Why do you think it is that you have to beat me to it, so to speak?

PT.: It's because I don't like the idea of your knowing more about me than I do myself. And I don't want you to surprise me with something I haven't already considered.

To prevent surprise is to prevent anxiety. If he has already thought of something, he has detoxified it and made himself immune.

THER.: And what sort of surprises do you fear?

PT.: One thing I wouldn't like to hear would be that I had feminine tendencies.

THER.: Why? What would that mean to you?

WHAT lies behind the resistance—anxiety about his masculinity-femininity—becomes a little clearer. An interpretation followed by matter-of-fact questions serves to modify the defense and permit an entry into a significant anxiety-laden area. The transference aspect of the patient's behavior is ignored, since the technique selected is sufficient for the time being to attenuate the resistance.

Interpositions and interpretations manage in the next example to remove an intercurrent resistance blocking the course of therapy.

FOR two or three interviews the therapist sensed a resistance increasing because of the patient's quality of speech. She spoke less and less of her conflict with her husband, spending most of the time talking about plans for a new house. In this hour nearly half the time has elapsed in which the patient has spoken only of rugs, drape colors, room measurements, etc. The therapist cannot fathom precisely what is being resisted, suspecting, of course, some new topic related to the husband and withheld because of the nature of the transference.

THER. (*interrupting*): I have the feeling you are telling me all these things about the house in order to avoid talking about some other thought on your mind.

The patient falls silent and fidgets.

THER.: What do you think?

PT.: You're right. I've been wanting to tell you for a week but dodged it. One thing about the marriage that I haven't mentioned yet is that I think I'm sexually frigid.

THER.: How so?

THE therapist does not stop to inquire why the patient resisted talking of her frigidity. Finding the topic now open with the patient's resistance lowered, he is content to continue investigation of the newly disclosed subject.

One particular form of resistance merits special consideration because it is so frequent and at times trying. That is, the resistance of silence. On page 55 the three common methods of handling the patient's silences were mentioned: (a) inquiring about the patient's immediate thoughts, (b) asking a direct question, and (c) waiting for him to continue. We can now add a fourth device—interpretation of the silence. In the beginning of therapy, with the patient becoming accustomed to the new situation, a few silences are to be expected. The first attempts to overcome them consist of active questioning and encouraging on the part of the therapist, with a gradual shifting of the responsibility to end the silence to the patient.

However, when silences become so frequent or prolonged that a question or other interposition is not sufficient to reinstitute the patient's flow of speech, interpretation of the silence is called for. As with other resistances, the therapist attempts to formulate what could be the content and motive of the resistance. If this can be done, a more specific plan of approach can be attempted. If not, more gentle tactics are utilized. The first example deals with a silence in the beginning of therapy, and the second with one in the middle stages.

1. IN contrast to the first two interviews when he talked volubly, this hour finds the patient almost dry of things to say. He appears edgy, looks here and there about the room, and at times acts a little grumpy.

He is a government clerk in the late twenties. He feels stifled and penned in by his job. Wanting to quit and try some other work, he fears the independent move. Yet the idea of staying in his present lowly job fills him with guilt, since he does possess above-average talents, particularly in music composition. The conflict is directly represented in his family set-up, in which his father stipulates that he should have a regular job while his mother encourages musical study.

The therapist tries a few questions which produce brief replies on the part of the patient. Waiting is also to no avail, since the patient tolerates the suspense in silence. Hence the therapist directly confronts the patient with his resistance.

THER.: Something seems to be blocking you today.

PT.: Guess so. I can't think of anything to say.

THER.: What do you think that means? You come to talk, but you don't have anything to say.

PT.: I don't know.

THER.: Maybe it's the expression of the part of you that has doubts about coming here.

PT.: That could be. I've wondered what can you do for me? Am I expecting some magic? I know you can't make up my mind for me. It's such a simple thing, too. Maybe I don't deserve to take up your time. I know you must have other cases more serious. Someone about to kill himself or fall apart. I don't have anything like that. When I talk about it, it sounds trivial.

THER.: You feel a little guilty about taking up my time?

PT.: I do. Maybe I shouldn't be here.

THER.: No. I'm interested in helping you. If this problem bothers you enough to come, then it isn't trivial.

ALREADY the transference fear of the therapist's unfavorable opinion develops. Clarification of the patient's feelings about therapy and a direct statement of professional dedication suffice to circumvent the resistance.

2. SEVERAL months of therapy have passed in the case of a hysterical woman suffering from arm and abdominal pains. She begins the hour with a few remarks about her job and then lapses into silence. Her manner and facial expression indicate her feelings of resentment.

THER.: What are you thinking about?
PT. (sullenly): Oh, nothing much.
THER.: You sound angry.
PT.: I am.
THER.: What are you mad about?
PT.: I didn't like your comment last time on my exaggerating things.

IN the previous interview she had told of manipulating her boy friend by threatening to kill herself unless he took her to the beach. One of her typical maneuvers is to heavily dramatize situations in order to get her way. The therapist had pointed out her mechanism of exaggerating the importance of her desires as an interpersonal weapon. At the time she agreed to the truth of the interpretation.

THER.: But you agreed with me last time.
PT.: I know it. But thinking about it later I didn't like it.
THER.: You felt I was reprimanding you?
PT.: No, not that. You were accusing me of being a phony. That's something I can't stand. Jerry says the same thing. He accuses me of always acting. Once we went to a party and . . . .

THE silence is broken and the patient continues to produce.

In the last two clinical examples, transference factors are evident in the functioning of the patient's presenting resistance. This is such a common phenomenon that the therapist should always give it thought when considering possible motives for all resistances. That the patient resists the verbalization of certain topics because of his anxiety over the therapist's possible reaction or opinion is understandable when we reflect on the origin of defense mechanisms in childhood. The child learns to outlaw as dangerous (incurring loss of love or physical punishment) certain impulses, behavior, and emotional expressions because of reactions they produce in his parents. Since the therapist grows in part of the patient's mind as a parent-figure, it is to be expected that censorships and avoidances will take place in relationships to the new parent-substitute as a representative of the original parent.

Hence, once a resistance is recognized, the therapist should look for its possible connection with himself. This rule serves to introduce the all-important subject of transferences into our consideration.

Transferences

First, let us discuss the definition and usages of the word "transference." The more specific and precise definition designates transference as the phenomenon in which a patient feels and behaves toward his therapist as he did toward important figures in his childhood (usually parents, siblings, or other relatives). Yet at times the term "transference" is loosely used to denote all the reactions of the patient toward the therapist. Actually this is a misuse of the word.

The patient's feelings toward the therapist are guided and determined in accordance with (a) his reality perception of the therapist's professional role, and (b) his past interpersonal experiences with significant family figures. At any given moment in therapy, the patient's orientation to the therapist represents a compounding of these two determinants with one or the other assuming reigning proportions. Reactions arising from (a) we consider appropriate to the present reality situation. For example, if the therapist openly insults the patient until he becomes angry, then the anger is not a transference but a normal emotional response appropriate to the situation. But if the patient is enraged because the therapist wears bow ties, then the disproportionate and inappropriate response signifies the presence of a transference.

Further uses of the word "transference" liken it to other terms. A "positive transference" means that in general the patient feels friendly towards the therapist and cooperates with him. "Negative transference" refers to the patient's resentment or unfriendly feelings which incline him to hinder or block the therapist's efforts. Again, these terms inadequately conceptualize the data observed in therapy. It would be more convenient to designate the relationship of specified intervals as friendly or unfriendly.

"Transference neurosis" has three usages of currency, referring to (a) a neurosis possessed by a patient capable of making transferences, (b) the transference phenomenon in its specific sense as defined above, and (c) an intensified form of the latter in which all of the patient's infantile conflicts are centered about the person of the therapist, a sort of galloping form of transference. I prefer to limit "transference neurosis" to the third category, designating the second simply as "transference."

A "transference improvement" consists of rapid amelioration of the patient's neurosis due to the particular nature and intensity of his transference onto the therapist. For example, a patient who equates neurosis with punishment for sins may give it up to win the approval awarded by a loving protector in the person of the re-edited parent, the therapist. A "transference aggravation" refers to an increase in the neurosis brought on by the type of transference made by the patient. For instance, if the patient anticipates physical contact with the therapist, the frustration of this desire may heighten her presenting symptoms.

In the following pages the word "transference" will be used to indicate the patient's acting toward the therapist as he did toward someone of significance in his past. Emphasis is placed on the patient's actions and behavior, verbal and nonverbal, because it is through the observation of these that the therapist recognizes the presence of a transference. Seldom does the patient flatly state spontaneously that he feels toward you as he felt about one of his parents, since, though he is conscious of his feelings, what they are a repetition of is outside his awareness. Rather as you listen to the patient's communications, observing connections between present and childhood experiences, a third set of experiences strikingly parallels the first two. That is, the patient in his relationship to the therapist, repeats and relives feelings that he had and has in other life areas. To aid the beginner in detecting the nature of a transference, common transference facts of observation are listed below.

The patient may think, feel, or act toward the therapist as if the latter were filling one of the following roles.

The Therapist as Giver of Affection.—Besides the therapist's realistic role of showing interest and understanding for the patient as a suffering person, further and less highly differentiated forms of affection may be sought by the patient. He may wish love in terms of praise, sympathy, pity, or direct expressions of being liked. To receive from the therapist smiles, encouragement, or simply words alone, regardless of content, may give him a lifting feeling of well-being equivalent to being loved. Conversely he may interpret the therapist's neutral facial expression or silence as an actual rejection.

Indications of this attitude are the patient's attempts to make the therapist laugh, frequent asking for suggestions or information, or appeals for sympathy by exaggerating the severity of unpleasant situations. He may bring gifts or do favors, hoping for a return of the thus-given affection. When desires for affection are frustrated, the therapist notes the patient's overreaction to a realistically slight rejection. For example, if a patient requests to be seen at a certain time and the therapist explains that he cannot because someone else has that hour, the patient may act and look severely hurt. Or he may feel intensely jealous of other patients and show his resentment by criticizing them or fuming at any interruption of his interview time by them. An extreme form of the expectation of affection from the therapist consists of desiring actual physical loving contact with him. Signals of such a desire are frank seductiveness by look and act, touching the therapist, or expressions of jealousy toward his wife who enjoys this intimacy.

The Therapist as Powerful Authority.—As the re-edition of a parent, the therapist takes over in the eyes of the patient attributes of strength and magic commonly ascribed by children to adults. Surrounded as he is in reality by the emblems (educational degrees and a title) of one type of authority in our culture, the therapist is predisposed to exaggerations of his power by the patient. To the patient a powerful authority who can reward, punish, and protect must be handled gingerly. Only things that can be pleasant must reach his ears. This authority must be cautiously sounded out for a long time in an effort to learn what areas can be demarcated as "safe" and "dangerous." If one succeeds in pleasing the potentate, he is rewarded by an invulnerable protection against anything bad happening. Of course a powerful figure, feared and respected, is also hated for the restrictions his assumed authoritarianism commands.

Such a view of the therapist by the patient can be deduced from several signs. The patient may be extremely agreeable and polite, always making his desires secondary to those of the therapist. For example, he will put himself to all kinds of trouble to choose an appointment time only slightly more convenient for the therapist. Or he will routinely call the therapist "sir" and submissively act as if he were dealing with an old man of world-famous importance. He may seek counsel on matters requiring wisdom and experience in fields unfamiliar to the therapist. He avoids expressing opinions—political, religious, social, etc.—which might disagree with those of the therapist and apologizes if one of his views might appear dissenting. All interpretations of the therapist (some of which must be wrong) are accepted as correct and final. If the therapist offers a view differing from one of the patient's, it is immediately adopted as of course true and how could he have been so stupid as to think otherwise. Later in therapy, he may make the accusation that he does not feel completely free in talking because of the therapist's censoring attitude.

The Therapist as Ideal Model.—The previously outlined role ascribed by the patient to the therapist may include or merge into the role of an admired, ideal model. The patient sees the therapist as a supertype—supremely intelligent, learned, all-knowing, properly balanced, etc. If he patterns himself after this model, he will thereby gain some of its qualities, i.e., strengths. By copying a supertype, one becomes a supertype himself and thus becomes safe and powerful against any threat.

Identifications with the therapist are easily observed. The patient may dress like him, adopt his manner of speech, walking, and posture, or take over one of his characteristic gestures. The therapist's tastes in books, pictures, furniture, etc., may be embraced. Interests and hobbies previously ignored by the patient may suddenly gain importance for him when he learns they are pastimes enjoyed by the therapist.

The Therapist as Rival.—In this type of transference the patient acts as if the therapist were someone with whom he is locked in a competitive struggle. He feels the therapist must in some part be fenced with, outmaneuvered, and defeated. Men, especially when close in age to the therapist, may see him as a rival intellectually, financially, or socially. Women may see him as a competitor in the male-female struggle who attempts to assert a masculine superiority.

Clues to such an attitude are found in the following behavior. The patient may try to test out by direct questions what and how much the therapist knows and has read. He may first interpret all his communications and, when the therapist manages to get in an interpretation, consistently say that he has already thought of that. At times he might feel out the therapist's memory of past interviews, hoping to catch him in an error. Or he may try to get the therapist to speak once he has learned that the therapist prefers silence most of the time . He may tell the therapist of one of his attitudes toward life and add challengingly that no one could ever influence it. Men ask about the therapist's economic success or the stage of his professional career. Women seek to establish the therapist's position on the roles women should have in the world or gauge his vulnerability to womanly wiles of charm and flirtation.

The Therapist as Favorite Child.—Strangely enough it often happens that the patient acts and feels as if the therapist were his child. At first this seems to contradict our idea that a transference is the repetition of a childhood attitude toward parents. But if we remember that many people seek their unattained ego ideals through the medium of a child and that these ego ideals were derived from their own parents to begin with, then it becomes understandable that the child really represents, once removed, a potential parent. The favorite child, if all goes well, will grow to become the idealized parent never achieved by the patient himself.

This phenomenon is particularly frequent when the patient is in fact older than the therapist. It does not necessarily lessen the therapist's powers to help, since the bright son is respected for his professional abilities. But in other aspects he becomes the object of protective mothering or fathering. For example, the patient may become solicitous about the therapist's health, instructing him to take better care of himself if he has a cold or warning him that he is working too hard. Women knit sweaters or bring food. Men offer advice about men's problems such as cars, investments, and business matters.

Throughout the course of psychotherapy, transferences contain one or the other of the five role-contents listed above. A transference seldom consists of one attitude in a pure form but is made up of a medley of these roles with one predominating at one time and some other at another. Also within a single hour the patient may react to the therapist as the embodiment of different figures. Hence it is more accurate to speak of a transference rather than the transference, since the content transferred undergoes shifts and changes.

Making Use of Transferences.—Once a transference is recognized, the therapist makes use of it in two ways. First by evaluating what transference role the patient is forming, the therapist gains understanding of what is being relived and re-experienced rather than being remembered. Secondly, the therapist may confront the patient with a transference to show him something he is unaware of or to overcome a resistance.

The manner in which a patient acts and feels about his therapist is a bonanza of psychological information. In subtracting the inappropriate from appropriate responses the therapist has a first-hand, immediately observable illustration of the patient's psychodynamics in an interpersonal relationship. For example:

1. A WOMAN from an old Southern family broke away in late adolescence from family ties and values. She became a nomadic Bohemian vigorously opposed to all authority. She expressed her feelings by zealous work in Anarchist societies and other radical movements. In therapy she often told of fearlessly challenging policemen and openly sneering at successful businessmen.

Yet her behavior toward the therapist was in marked contrast to this. She was very respectful, nonaggressive and acquiescent—all attitudes she faintly remembers having as a child toward her parents until adolescence. The therapist's concept was that the patient unconsciously saw him as a feared and loved parent who must not be antagonized. She really feared authority as a source of punishment. Later in therapy this was confirmed by the fact that though she proudly told everyone else, she was unable for months to tell the therapist that her lover was a Negro.

2. JAILED for stealing, a tough adolescent boy snarled and wisecracked at all adults. A major event in his past life was the war death of an older brother noted for his kindness toward the patient. On meeting the therapist, the boy showed his usual bored nonchalance. For a few minutes he gave clipped answers to questions about his age, school grade, etc. Then spontaneously he added:

PT.: You know, it was my birthday yesterday.
THER.: And did anyone remember you?

SUDDENLY the patient burst into tears and sobbed heavily. From this moving transference reaction the therapist can see beneath the insouciant façade elements which do not appear in a routine psychiatric history.

The second use made by the therapist of a transference is in regulating the future course of therapy. In a mainly supportive therapy the patient is shown few if any aspects of his transferences. Transferences may be allowed to continue to increase defensive processes (cf. page 153). In an uncovering therapy the patient is shown those aspects of his transferences essential for his understanding of important neurotic conflicts. Of all the interpretations made in psychotherapy none carries greater weight in modifying defenses than a correct transference interpretation confronting the patient with the motivations of his thoughts and feelings for the therapist.

When is the patient shown his transference? The question of timing is answered by a rule of considerable value. That is, a transference is not discussed until a strong resistance is met. As long as the patient continues to talk freely about important problems with a minimum of resistance, the transference or transferences are left untouched. But when the patient becomes blocked or side-tracked in his efforts, discussion of his feelings about the therapist is in order.

The clinical examples on pages 98 and 105 illustrated how the patient may erect defenses around certain topics because of his emotions toward the therapist. Since it proved sufficient to overcome the presenting resistance, the factor of the therapist in those examples was hardly touched upon. In the following example the nature of his transference is more extensively unfolded to the patient.

An intelligent adolescent boy is undergoing psychotherapy in an effort to relieve his confusion over sexual and religious matters which bear on a rift with his parents. He is of a friendly, outgoing nature but sensitive to the slightest criticism.

It came to light in therapy that he is particularly intrigued and excited by men's hair. This began at the age of four when he first saw his father's pubic hair and genitals. Nowadays head or pubic hair fascinates him. A few months before therapy he had fantasies of stealing hair shampoo from drug stores. He was conscious that it had some relationship to his father's use of shampoo, a habit denied him by parental edict.

In therapy one of the patient's characteristics is to say teasingly, "I'm thinking of something but I can't bear to say it." Until now this trait has been ignored by the therapist, since the patient usually went right on to another topic. However, at this point in therapy the trait has swelled to the size of a major resistance. The patient is silent, occasionally looks at the therapist expectantly, and repeats, "I just can't say it, I just can't say it." The therapist has the feeling that the patient is fencing tauntingly, that he is not really experiencing a painful affect in connection with his thought content. Finally the patient continues:

Pt.: You know I thought of stealing again the other day. This time it involved you. When I was downtown I thought of stealing the *Saturday Review* from the newsstands.

Ther.: Why the *Saturday Review*?

Pt.: That is where you come in. I had never seen it before until I saw it in your waiting room. It's sort of an intellectual magazine. Maybe I thought I'd be an intellect, too.

Ther.: It's interesting that of the two things you've wanted to steal, the first involves your father and the second me.

Pt.: You mean I think you're a father to me?

Ther.: Maybe. At least we see that you want something I have just as you wanted something your father had. You compete with me as you do with your father. Even in the interview here you struggle with me, like in holding back to see what I'll do about it.

A transference is actually a resistance in the sense that something is re-enacted or relived with the therapist rather than being recalled and verbalized to him. Two common forms of resistance repeatedly requiring transference interpretations arise when (a) the patient avoids a topic easily seen by the therapist as related to him and (b) the patient becomes interested in talking only of his feelings concerning the therapist.

In the case of (a), the therapist can initiate a discussion of the patient's feelings about him. As these feelings are revealed as motives for the avoidance, the therapist can begin to demonstrate to the patient their unrealistic basis in terms of ascribing one's own qualities to someone else or as literally transferring attributes from a historically important person to the therapist. When the patient with a sufficient reality sense understands this mechanism, the resistance diminishes and the topic being defended becomes available for investigation, as in what follows:

ONE day an outwardly majestic actress alternately paused and rambled during the interview in contrast to her previous smooth and relevant flow. In the past few interviews her usually seductive behavior toward the therapist has become in little ways increasingly more enticing. After a long silence, the therapist approaches the transference.

THER.: It seems you are having some difficulty talking today.
PT.: It does, doesn't it? I know I must try to be honest and tell you everything, but sometimes it's so hard. I don't know quite how to go about it. (*Silence.*)
THER.: Is it something to do with me?
PT. (*laughs*): It is. I think the main thing that bothers me is how you will take it. Not that you will do anything about it. I know by now that you won't laugh at me. But you will think this is so childish.
THER.: Why would I?
PT.: It's something anyone would think a grown woman should have gotten over by now. Once a few years ago I told my

mother about it and she scorned me, saying I sounded like a bobby-soxer.

THER.: And you're afraid I will react like your mother?

PT.: It's silly to feel that way, I know. Well, what it is is a day-dream I've had for years. In it I think of myself as a queen like Cleopatra who is surrounded by a sort of harem of big, handsome men. All these men are my slaves. Some are in chains. They do anything I want them to. For the first time a couple of weeks ago you were one of the men.

THE therapist's interpretations, bringing out in the open the basis for her difficulty in speaking and indicating that she fears him as she learned to fear her mother, enables the patient to reveal an important fantasy which includes further transference material.

When the patient's resistance takes the form of his talking only about the therapist as in (b), whether in friendly or unfriendly terms, again the therapist must initiate an exploration of the phenomenon and its defensive purpose. The next example illustrates how this may be done.

FOR almost half of an interview the patient exhaustively expresses her admiration and near-love for the therapist. During this time in therapy she is considering separating from her husband, who she feels is intolerant and lacking in human understanding. So much of her attention is devoted to her praise of the therapist that she says nothing about the outcome of a marital argument unfinished at the time of the last interview.

At this moment she is describing further glorious things she has heard from friends about the therapist.

THER.: And no one had anything bad to say?

PT.: No. Or maybe I wouldn't let them. To me you are perfect.

THER.: But nobody could be so perfect as the person you describe.

PT.: I admit you must have faults, but I haven't found any. Even if you do, your understanding makes up for them. You're the only one who really understands me.

THER.: And it's this not being understood that angers you about your husband?

PT.: Yes. He's terrible. What I want is a man who understands that people have feelings and are not just machines. In fact I've thought it would be nice to be married to you. You are the only one who has ever been interested in me.

THER.: But I'm paid to be interested in people, it's my job.

PT.: I know. Still I think you would make me a fine husband.

THER.: If I were your husband, who would be your psychiatrist?

PT.: I wouldn't need one.

THER.: Why not?

PT.: Then I'd be all right. I wouldn't have to go through all this talking and questioning.

THER.: Maybe in one sense that's what making me your husband means. I couldn't be objective about you, it would take away my power as a therapist.

PT.: That comes close to something I once thought—if we were together you'd be on my level, not over me, and you couldn't pry into my life as you do now. Maybe I'd be telling you instead of you telling me.

THER.: Like your husband now?

PT.: You mean that I want to snare you like I snared him. You may be right.

THE therapist succeeds in partially showing the patient that she repeats in her transference what she does with her husband and that hidden beneath her admiration of the therapist lie other less friendly motives.

Throughout psychotherapy each patient makes several transferences, the therapist representing now one figure, now another. The multiplicity and extent of these reactions depend greatly upon whether the therapist allows them to develop. Indeed it must be kept in mind that in some reality respects the therapist is like a parent especially when he may guide, suggest, and reassure. For example, suggesting to the patient that he postpone an important decision in a matter that could bring him unpleasant consequences is actually a parent-like function. Hence not all of the patient's reactions are transferences. Some are appropriate and proportionate to the therapist's realistic role.

Allowing transferences to develop means behaving as much as possible as a professional helper in an accepting, noncritical, nonmoralizing manner. If the therapist is knowingly or unknowingly critical, then the patient is justified in behaving toward him as if he were a punishing parent and the opportunity for the patient to make this kind of a transference as a projection out of his own mind is unfortunately lost. "Manipulating" the transference in the sense of playing like a "pally" father or a loving mother is to be avoided in an uncovering therapy. To become convinced that his transference feelings are spontaneous creations of his own mind, the patient must have minimum reality justification for their nature.

Working Through

The process of repeated verbalization by the patient and interpretation by the therapist of central neurotic conflicts is called "working through." Over and over, now here in one area and there in another, important defenses and their motivations are brought into the patient's consciousness. A major resistance or defense is seldom undone by one interpretation or even by the activities of one interview. Dynamic, structural, and economic changes in neurotic processes are the result of weeks and months of working through.

Several mechanisms operate in working through, both in and outside the therapeutic interviews. First, in the interview recollection, reconstruction, re-experiencing and repetition take place. Recollection means the production of memories by the patient. These memories arise in accordance with what is being experienced *in the present* by the patient in an interpersonal relationship with the therapist or someone else. It is the task of the therapist when listening to the patient's recollections to try to correlate them with the present, with the transference situation and with other memories. This is usually done in the therapist's mind by listening for themes and patterns, which are easier to formulate, remember, and match than individual memory details, as in the following example:

THE patient is complaining that her boy friend is very stingy. They are often treated to dinner by other couples, but he does not offer to return the gesture. Now she is embarrassed whenever she meets these friends, feeling that they must look down on her for having such a man. She recalls a couple of other men in her life who were the same way. In fact in the case of one of them his miserliness resulted in her leaving him.

The therapist remembers that the theme of the previous interview was the generosity of a man who had befriended the patient. The theme of the two interviews then is "what men give and what men take." In his own thinking the therapist next relates this theme to the transference situation at the moment to see how the patient might view him in terms of giving and taking.

Reconstruction is the deduction of what the patient must have thought or felt at a time which he cannot recall clearly but about which he can give some data. The therapist and often the patient himself can make reconstructions based on knowledge of general human behavior. For example, a patient cannot recall what she thought when, at age eight, she first saw her father's erect penis but states, "It must have been a surprise and a shock, because the only male genital I had seen before was my baby brother's and I know such a sight would be shocking to a little girl."

Re-experiencing involves reliving feelings and behavior once experienced toward an important figure of the past. A transference is a re-experiencing. Of course, the phenomenon takes place to some extent in all interpersonal relationships, not only the therapeutic one.

Repetition means the frequent recurrence of all these mechanisms, including their interpretation by the therapist. Knowing that effective work requires the application of force over a period of time, the therapist patiently and repeatedly employs his techniques with versatility. By versatility I mean that the therapist shows some resourcefulness and suppleness in pointing out the same thing in many different ways. He avoids belaboring the patient with the same statement (e.g., "you are dependent") over and over until it becomes a chant. While the therapist slowly chips away at fragments of neuroses, the patient undergoes literally hundreds of modifying learning experiences.

Outside the therapeutic hours a working through goes on in that the patient repeatedly thinks of things he has learned and tests them out on himself in his life experiences. Processes for which we have no better terms than absorption, assimilation, and consolidation lead to the cumulative effects produced by dynamic uncovering psychotherapy.

Typical Use of Techniques

A sector from a clinical case is now presented to illustrate some typical techniques utilized in the middle of therapy.

OUR patient is a mannerly woman in her mid-twenties. She comes for help because of generalized feelings of depression and dissatisfaction both with her job and her marriage. Working full time for low pay as a secretary, she gloomily sees no chance for a better financial future. This impinges on her relationship to her husband, who also earns little and who cannot keep a steady job. Even more upsetting is his heavy drinking. Two or three nights a week and every week end he drinks himself into a helpless stupor. All efforts on the part of the patient to help him stop drinking have failed. In fact he claims that it is her attitude toward him that makes him drink all the more. He refuses to consult a psychiatrist about his alcoholism, saying that it is entirely a matter of his own free choice whether he drinks or not. The patient suffers from conflicting thoughts whether to break up the marriage or try to keep it going.

Her background was that of a small-town girl growing up in a farming area in the West. Her parents were hard-working, religious people of the soil concerned with the immediacies of survival. She feels that she and her brother, five years younger, were raised in a fair and kindly spirit, her only criticism being that her father kept himself aloof from the jolly, rough-and-tumble play she saw carried on by other fathers with their children. On graduating from high school, she left home for a job in the city. First a clerk, she studied nights and advanced to a position as secretary in the company she works for at present. Three years ago she met her husband, at that time also employed by this company, and, after six months' courtship, they married. The husband drank only socially when she first knew him, but in the past two years he has become increasingly alcoholic.

Therapy thus far has consisted mainly of an expression of her feelings about the job and her husband, with some clarification of the second problem as being primary. The clinical diagnosis is a reactive depression complicating a character neurosis. The working dynamic diagnosis concerns the patient's orientation toward men, her husband in particular, and her participant role in a symbiosis with an alcoholic. Up to this point in therapy the therapist's remarks have consisted mainly of interpositions with an occasional comment to the effect that she feels protective as well as resentful toward her husband. The next five interviews are given in some detail.

Interview 15.

TODAY the patient is talking about many of the little habits and mannerisms her husband (John) has which irritate her. He never can sit still, he is always making some kind of noise with his mouth or nose, and he is inattentive about his clothes.

PT.: His clothes are a sore spot with us. He never cleans or brushes them. If I'd let him, he would wear the same suit for days. I have to get after him constantly to change his underwear. And he never likes to buy a new suit. We are going down tomorrow to get him a new suit. He hasn't had one in years.

THER.: You go with him when he buys his clothes?

PT.: Yes. I don't trust him. He'd pick out something horrible. That's why I always buy his socks and ties. He has no taste in clothes. He likes bright colors, like yellow ties and green socks. He tries to look flashy, but he's not the flashy type at all.

THER.: Does he object to your picking out his clothes?

PT.: No. He seems to like it. Once in a while he used to squawk, but now he accepts it. Other things that I do annoy him, though. Like meals. He doesn't eat much, and he likes things that are bad for him—hot dogs and pie. I try to see that he has a balanced diet, fruit and vegetables. Yesterday we planned to have dinner at six. About four-thirty we went past a hot-dog stand and he wanted one. I told him it would spoil his appetite for dinner. He blew up, said I never let him have his own way. He's right as far as eating goes. But I do it for his own good.

HER concern over the husband's clothes and food and the way she dominates him "for his own good" point to her concept of him as a child requiring her motherly care. The therapist makes a clarification interpretation in the form of a question.

THER.: It seems you are very worried about his diet. Are you afraid he will get sick?

PT.: Yes, I am. John is quite thin and gets colds easily. And his drinking. I've read that if you drink a lot and don't eat the right things you're liable to get liver cirrhosis or a vitamin deficiency. God, we had a terrible time the other night. He came home drunk and kept on drinking. I didn't say anything to him about it because I'm beginning to see that it's hopeless. I can't do anything about it. He kept on drinking bourbon and stumbling around. I went to bed. About three o'clock I woke up and he still hadn't come to bed. So I went into the kitchen and he was lying there out cold. I tried to drag him but he's too heavy. He came to a little and pushed me away. He wanted to walk by himself. Now I know what they mean by "blind drunk." He just couldn't see things. He'd crash right into a table, fall down, get up again and smack into the door. Finally he let me put him to bed. When he gets that bad he's just like a helpless baby.

THER.: Maybe that gets close to your feeling about him when he's sober, too. Buying clothes for him, looking after what he eats, protecting him from sickness—those are all things that mothers do for their children.

PT. (*hesitantly*): Yes. I suppose so. Although I don't want to be a mother to him. Another thing that happens is, he gets so drunk that he's still drunk in the morning and can't go to work. That's why he can't hold a job. He doesn't show up regularly and they fire him.

THE initial confrontation apparently does not sink in. She is hesitant to accept it and moves away from it in another direction. However, such understandings develop slowly and in small steps. The opportunity will arise again to show her this aspect of her marital relationship. The therapist's next question keeps her close to the general mother-child area.

THER.: Do you get breakfast for him when he's drunk in the morning?

PT.: Sometimes I leave orange juice for him to drink. Usually I'm so furious when he doesn't get up for work that I just leave. What burns me up is that I have to get up to go to work so that we'll have enough money to get by on.

SHE then continues to speak of their financial problems and his irresponsibility in money matters. She doesn't trust him to run a checking account and pays all the bills herself. More and more a picture of this marriage develops in which, while he appears as the weak and submissive child bitterly taking refuge in the infantile oblivion of alcohol, she is the strong, managing, and domineering mother-figure. The interaction of the personality configurations of this couple illustrates how neurotic processes are shared. The problem for therapy is showing her her contribution to the symbiotic drama without accusingly attacking her self-esteem. Of greatest value will be her involvement of the therapist in a transference similar to the relationship with her husband.

Interview 16.

PT.: What you said last time about being a mother to John struck me. I was thinking about it afterwards . . .

Testimony that the seemingly dismissed interpretation of the last interview had an impact and echo.

PT.: . . . how that works. I do treat him like a child. Then I was thinking about other men I knew before I was married. Something of the same happened there. For instance, I went with a fellow for about two years. My girl friend said he was a mouse and that I led him around by the nose. At the time I couldn't see it, but I can now. He used to like to go fishing, but I hated it, so we always did what I wanted to do on week ends. I had to teach him how to dance and how to act in a restaurant.

SHE continues to describe this relationship, which in many ways parallels the present one to her husband. The man was passive, submissive, and eager to please her. She finally sent him away because he seemed too weak and clinging for her to marry. She then takes up the topic of her ideal man.

PT.: All my life I had a clear picture of the kind of man I would like to marry. He is a tall, strong, clean-cut type, very successful and very intelligent. In my day-dreams I would meet him at a party, he would pay more attention to me than to any of the others, and eventually he would become completely devoted. I always liked the idea of a man doing all sorts of the little conventional things you see in the movies—bringing flowers, presents, surprise trips.
THER.: Did you ever meet anyone who filled this ideal?
PT.: Only once. About a year ago we met a couple at a bridge club we belong to. He seemed like a god to me, but he mostly ignored me. Somehow I always knew I'd never really get such a dream man.

THER.: You wanted a strong man, but you always wound up with weak ones.

A comparison interpretation contrasting her wish-fantasy with her reality behavior.

PT.: Yes, that's right. I know it can't be coincidental. I must attract weak ones. I know that I feel sure of myself with men like my husband when I first meet them. Maybe I can tell that they are drawn to me. Or maybe that I can run them around. That's a horrible way to be. I used to laugh at women who nagged their men, but I guess I'm just as bad. (*Weeps.*)

THE therapist waits for her to regain control of her feelings. When she is able to speak again, he asks a question designed to elucidate the marital relationship.

THER.: When you first met your husband, was he immediately drawn to you?
PT.: In a way. He worked in the same office I did. We started having lunch together . . . .

IT develops that at first the patient did not feel her future husband to be the child he seems now. He was a witty, lively sort of person who amused her greatly. Once sexual intercourse began, she found it more pleasurable than she had ever experienced before. This to her was proof that it would be a happy marriage.

PT.: In the past year all that has disappeared. We haven't had any sexual relations for six months and before that only about once a month.
THER.: Does your husband object to this?

Looking to see if she controls him in this respect also.

PT.: No. It seems to suit him. He doesn't say anything about it.
THER.: And does such a period of abstinence bother you at all?
PT.: No. I seem to have lost my sexual interest. Even during

my periods which used to be the time I was most excited, I don't feel it any more. Once in awhile I do feel affectionate toward John. Then I hug him or hold him in bed. But that's usually when I feel sorry for him, when I know he's sick emotionally and can't help himself. It's pity I feel, and you can't feel sexually toward someone you have only pity for.

THER.: Nor toward a sick child. We must stop there for today, our time is up.

THE therapist ends the hour with a repetition of the mother-child interpretation, proposing the absence of intercourse as further evidence for this concept.

Interview 17.

THE patient begins this hour by speaking of one of her friends at work. Together they criticize various aspects of the way the company office is operated. Also they confide in one another about their personal problems. The friend is unmarried and gets an allowance from her parents. Thus she is able to spend quite a bit of money on her clothes and personal belongings. She often gives the patient gifts of perfume or jewelry. Not only does this embarrass the patient, who cannot reciprocate, but it angers her in that the friend's largesse emphasizes her own limited funds, most of which are spent on rent, food, and household needs.

All this the therapist listens to without interposition or interpretation, waiting for an opportunity to take up the thread of the previous interview. It comes in connection with a dream.

PT.: I had a dream last night that I can remember clearly. Usually I can't remember them the next day. It was about dogs. I was standing in a large field. Across the field I could see a dog—an Irish setter—coming through the grass. When he got closer I could see that he, or I guess it must be she, was carrying a little puppy in her mouth. It was a mother dog and her puppy. The puppy was sick I imagined, because his nose was running and he was being carried. Otherwise he could have walked.

DREAMS are used in psychotherapy but not fully interpreted in the manner characteristic of psychoanalysis. For example, in psychoanalysis the analyst would attempt to get associations to as many elements in this dream as possible, i.e., track down the detailed thought connection of why it is an *Irish* setter, what a field means, etc. But in psychotherapy the therapist uses the dream as if it were any other type of material presented by the patient. He tries to sort out a theme or pattern in it which relates to the past, present, or transference and then, if the patient's learning state (resistance) is suitable, points out the theme for further discussion. The technique used here at this moment is a typical one.

THER.: So the dream is about a mother dog and her sick child.

PT.: Of course it must refer to me and John. We've talked about my being a mother and he a child.

THER.: And he gets a lot of colds with a running nose?

PT.: Yes. I wonder why I dreamed about dogs. We don't have a dog. I was thinking of getting one, but then there's no one home in the daytime to take care of him. A dog is like a child. Maybe the dream is about that, too. I always wanted to have children, but now I'm not so sure. I'd never try to raise a child with John the way he is now.

THER.: How is it that you haven't become pregnant?

PT.: I was pregnant once before I was married and had an abortion. But you mean with John. At first we didn't even talk about having children. I don't know why. When I got to know him better, I got the feeling that he didn't want to have children. When I brought the subject up, he'd say we couldn't afford it or we didn't have enough room in the apartment. But I could tell that he really didn't like children. Sometimes we visit a neighbor who has children, and John ignores them. He won't play with them or talk to them. Says they're noisy brats who don't know their place.

THER.: So you haven't tried to get pregnant?

PT.: No. Now, of course, I'm not even sure I want to stay with John. This would be no time to have a baby. Maybe I've always sensed that. I think I know what it is. He would be jealous of a baby. A baby would take away some of the attention I give him.

THER.: A baby would be a rival for your motherly care.

HERE a working-through is taking place. Repeated consideration and interpretation of a central mechanism help to fix it in the patient's consciousness. The dream has served its purpose in reopening the mother-child topic. Its relationship to the patient's pregnancy wishes and concepts is left unexamined.

PT.: I'm sure that's what he feels underneath. And he's right. I couldn't spend as much time with him.

THER.: You say you always thought of yourself as having children?

Exploring the strength of her need to have a child or a child substitute.

PT.: I began to think of having children when I was about fourteen. All my girl friends would spend hours talking about how many children we would have and what kind. I wanted three, two boys and a girl. I imagined just what they'd look like, where they would go to school, what they would become, and so forth.

THER.: And your imagined husband was the ideal man?

PT.: That's odd. I never even thought what their father would be like. My picture of an ideal man came later when I was about sixteen or seventeen.

How the adolescent idea of children without a father might relate to the pregnancy and abortion mentioned in passing is not explored. Such interesting by-paths must often remain untrod.

Interview 18.

AFTER only a few minutes have gone by, the therapist is aware of the presence of an intercurrent resistance. Instead of speaking freely and evenly on a specific topic, the patient appears uncertain and backward. She meanders from subject to subject, and her comments are punctuated with silences of atypical length. She overelaborates minutiae and makes no mention of her presenting problems or the material of the preceding interviews.

PT.: I don't know what to talk about today. (Pause.) The other day I learned something interesting. I always like to learn new things. A friend and I were talking about baking. I brought up the fact that I've never learned how to make a pie. She offered to show me, so we went to her place. It's really very simple. First you make the dough. . . .

SHE gives in detail each step of pie-making. The therapist attempts to circumvent the resistance with a leading question but he is unsuccessful.

PT.: . . . it came out pretty well. I'm going to try it at home my next day off.

THER.: Does your husband like pies?

PT.: Not especially. He doesn't pay much attention to what he eats. (*Pause.*) Then I saw my other girl friend, the one at work. She and I plan to go to a lecture together on psychology. She was the one who first became interested in psychology and psychiatry. She went to a lecture series and then began doing some reading. One day I saw a book on psychiatry on her desk. From then on it was our favorite topic of conversation. (*Long silence.*)

THER.: What are you thinking about?

PT. (*uneasy*): Something I read in one of the books. I can't remember which one. I liked the one by S. the best. It made a lot of sense to me. (*Silence.*)

THER.: You seem to have some trouble talking today.

PT.: I know. I was sure you'd notice it. I don't hide it very well when there's something I find hard to talk about.

THER.: Why is it hard?

PT.: I don't know. It just is.

MEETING a resistance, the therapist wonders first about its motive and content in terms of the transference. A further clue is that it has some association with her reading in psychiatry, an activity bound to have bearing on the therapeutic relationship. Hence the therapist gently shakes the transference tree to see what falls.

THER.: Maybe it's hard because it has something to do with me.

PT.: You're right. I read that in psychotherapy the patient has to tell all her feelings, even those toward the therapist. At the time I didn't think much about it. But when I began coming here I soon found out how hard that is. Lately, maybe because we've been talking about my treating a man as if he were a child, I've noticed that I have that tendency toward you. Actually I have two separate feelings about you. One is that you are some sort of superman, perfect, always right. But the other is opposite to it. Not that you are really a child, but I feel motherly toward you. Days when you look tired I wonder if you are getting enough rest. Or when you cough I think maybe you are getting a cold and shouldn't sit in this cold room.

ILLUSTRATING a mixture of transferences. Her image of the therapist contains elements of powerful-authority, ideal-model, and favorite-child transference. Noteworthy is the fact that her view of the therapist represents a composite of the two men in her life, the fantasied ideal and the reality weakling. That the patient is talking at her normal pace again and is developing a topic, indicates the diminution of the particular resistance. Since the patient, by herself, is coming closer to an understanding of the parallel between therapist and husband, the therapist does not interrupt.

PT.: Of course my feeling that you should take better care of yourself is maternal. And, as you pointed out once, this is how I react toward John. I'm always worrying about his health. There's no reason I should worry about you. A doctor certainly knows how to take care of himself.
THER.: Especially if he is a superman.
PT. (laughs): I almost forgot that. It's a funny mixture. How can a superman be a child who needs a mother? Maybe I think that underneath all men are children.

To himself the therapist thinks of the possibility that she wishes to make men children, reduce a superman to the status of a child. Obviously it is no time to interpret such an impulse. The evidence is still scanty, and it must gradually be approached from the standpoint of defense rather than wish. In the next interview a chance for a wish-defense interpretation presents itself.

Interview 19.
PT.: After last time I gave a lot of thought to that point about how men are children to me....

The extra-interview working through of reflection.

PT.: . . . I had a good example happen to me yesterday. One of
the men where I work was trying to look up something in the
files. He looked as if he didn't know what he was doing. To
me, anyway, he looked puzzled. As I went over to help him
I said laughingly to one of the other girls, "It's all too com-
plicated for the poor boy." When I got there I found out he
knew as much about the files as I did. He had found a mistake in them and that's why he was having trouble. But I
thought of him as a confused little boy whom I would have
to help. That was my first reaction, so it must be a strong
desire in me to think of men as children who need me.

THE patient goes on to another example involving a young man
she was briefly engaged to. Again she is able now to see many of
the mother-child aspects of this relationship. Then she begins to
talk about her husband in terms of this theme.

PT.: Two more things came to me about treating John as a child,
a little boy. The first is not just treating him as one but in a
way keeping him one. A few months ago he wanted to enlist
in the Army. He thinks a war is coming and he would be
drafted anyway. If he enlists he'd have a better job. But I
thought of all sorts of reasons to talk him out of it. All the
time I knew he wanted to be a soldier to see if he could be
more of a man, a man among men and not a weakling doing
women's work like clerking. (Pause.)
THER.: You said there were two things in this regard. What was
the other?

An interposition to keep the patient going.

PT.: The other was when he wanted to grow a moustache. I had
heard other women protesting about their husbands' growing
a moustache and I laughed at them because I knew that they
didn't like their husbands to assert their masculinity. But
when John started it I was the same way. I poked fun at him
for trying to be something he wasn't. I shamed him out of it.
I kept him a boy, wouldn't let him do what men like to do.

THER.: Why are you afraid of letting him be a man, more asser-
tive?

A WISH-DEFENSE interpretation made from the defense side.   The
therapist does not begin by pointing to her wish to weaken, fetter,
and hamstring her husband but to her anxiety over his becoming
strong and indomitable.   Later the wish will be approached.

PT.: I'm not sure.   Maybe I want to be the boss.   Or maybe I'm
afraid he would give me a bad time.
THER.: In what way?
PT.: Leave me?   I don't know.

As yet the childhood derivation of her relationship to men is
unknown.   The roles of the younger brother, father, and mother
in determining her outlook during her formative years await discussion.   Eventually the most effective interpretation of her behavior will show her the repetition of a childhood motif in her
orientation to both husband and therapist.

We come now to the end stages of therapy.   The next
chapter concerns the several techniques available to the
therapist for bringing therapy to a close.

Chapter 8

ENDING THE THERAPY

We must admit that it is exceedingly difficult to set up general criteria which decide when therapy should terminate. Absence of symptoms, freedom from work, social, or sexual inhibitions, and the giving and receiving of love with a loved partner are all theoretical goals whose achievement indicates that therapy can end. Few, if any, patients reach this ideal. In practice, the therapist attempts only to accomplish a limited aim which differs from patient to patient. It may be the relief of a compulsion, or it may be a better marital adjustment with the compulsion remaining. For each individual patient the therapist has a particular goal in mind commensurate with the intensity of the patient's presenting problem and his psychological resources in allying with the therapeutic effort to overcome it.

Sometimes in the middle of therapy the therapist can more precisely assess whether the anticipated goal (known only to him, of course) can be reached. These predictions cannot compare in accuracy with those of an astronomer, but they easily rival most of the weatherman's. Whether the therapeutic goal is reached or not, ending situations can be divided into two groups: (a) those in which the patient himself wishes to stop or must because of external circumstances; and (b) those in which, cured or not, the patient wishes to continue therapy.

At times the patient must conclude therapy because he is moving to another city or his job makes it impossible for him to keep regular appointments. No special maneuvers are necessary in bringing treatment to a close. The last few interviews are handled like those of the middle stages, with the exception that topics requiring extensive interpretations and the working-through of further interviews are not entered into.

Since symptoms or unpleasant life situations brought on by the patient's personality are the propelling fuels of therapy, with their amelioration or removal the patient often expresses a desire to stop coming. This may represent a realistic decision, or it may be the expression of strong resistances against further uncovering. In either case, the pros and cons of the patient's desire are discussed like any other decision. A realistic decision is naturally agreed with. But it is important for the therapist to understand that, even when the patient's motive is a defensive one, if the desire to end survives after discussion, it should not be subjected to an altering interpretive force.

In psychotherapy the therapist should neither induce the patient to undertake treatment nor talk him into continuing it. If the patient is convinced that he wishes to stop, the therapist can only concur and not tamper with the defense. Should the patient have doubts, they can be the subject of further interviews until he decides for himself. The patient made the decision in the following example:

FOLLOWING the loss of her fiancé in an auto accident two years previous to coming to therapy, a woman became depressed, with the typical symptoms of withdrawal, loss of interest, fatigue, etc. After some twenty hours of psychotherapy she began to improve, going to parties and dances and seeing old boy friends. The lift in her mood, however, was not the result of insight into the mechanisms of her depression. Therapy had been mainly supportive, since it soon became evident that strong defenses were operating against the therapeutic process. The specific elements involved in the transference improvement could not be clearly elucidated.

At the present interview the patient expresses her desire to end therapy.

Pt.: I feel so much better these days I think I'm about over it. I really don't see any reason why I should come back, do you?

Ther.: No. If you're feeling better and seem to have recovered, there's no need for us to continue. Why don't we meet one more time, and if everything continues well for you then, we can stop.

The therapist does not put pressure on her but agrees with the resistance. Though he may suspect the patient is leaving to avoid approaching her transference feelings, no mention is made of it.

As long as the patient has shown improvement for what-ever covering or uncovering reasons, and wishes to stop, ending therapy is in order. It is by no means necessary that the patient or even the therapist have a complete under-standing of the dynamics of the neurosis or of the improve-ment. Such a goal of academic perfection would make psychotherapy interminable.

Ending when the patient, improved or not, wishes to continue is at times more difficult. Certain patients, even when freed of their presenting problem, like to go on in therapy for a variety of reasons: to bask in the noncritical atmosphere of the interview, to have a pleasant conversation with a loved or admired figure, etc. But if the therapist sincerely feels that as much has been therapeutically accom-plished as is possible and the patient gives no indication of wishing to stop, then it is up to him to suggest termination. Such a decision on the part of the therapist must be tem-pered with the understanding that neurotic processes are not easily or quickly changed. A patient suitable for uncovering therapy should be given a prolonged opportunity, perhaps two or three years, to work toward improvement.

Suggesting an ending when the patient wants to continue requires tact and firm sincerity. Knowing that the patient will, in some part, take the move as a personal rejection, the therapist proceeds slowly and in small stages. With extremely sensitive patients the topic can be introduced weeks or months before the actual ending to allow them to become acclimated to the idea. One method of doing this is shown in the following example:

AFTER eight months of therapy, a housewife has been free of anxiety attacks for almost two months. She shows no interest in discontinuing therapy. The therapist feels that the goal he had in mind at the beginning has been reached and little more can be accomplished. He approaches the subject of terminating.

THER.: Now, I think we should give some thought to the idea of ending treatment. You seem to be getting along well these days.

PT.: But do you think I'll continue that way if I stop now?

THER.: I see no reason why not.

PT.: Well, I'm not sure I'd like to stop right now.

THER.: We don't have to stop immediately. Let's just keep it in mind. Another thing we might consider is that you come once a week for a while and see how it goes.

PT.: That would be all right with me.

THE therapist indicates his feeling that therapy should end but allows the patient to break off gradually by diminishing the frequency of the continued interviews.

The patient may have some anxiety or dissatisfaction from losing a supporting relationship on which he has become dependent. These advents are discussed, interpreted, and worked through like any other material in therapy.

When the patient is only slightly improved or is unimproved after prolonged therapy but wishes to continue, again the therapist has the frequently awkward task of bringing about an ending. When the therapist recognizes that little more can be done, he can begin to help the patient accept the situation without imparting the feeling that all is hope·less. For example:

1. AFTER almost two years of twice-a-week psychotherapy which at first seemed to offer a good prognosis for the patient, a woman with a hysterical character, the therapist realizes that her personality structure is irreversible. Supportive and uncovering efforts to modify her infantile impulsiveness and crisis-producing theatrical behavior have failed. In spite of this the patient wants to go on. The therapist honestly states his views.

THER.: I really feel that we have done about as much as we can. Some of these things are just too deep-seated and complex to work out.

PT. (distressed): But what am I going to do about them if this treatment doesn't work?

THER.: It isn't as bad as all that. I think you can work on some of the things you've learned about yourself here. If you put some of it to use, I'm sure it will help you.

PT.: Is this our last interview?

THER.: Oh, no. Let's talk a few more times and tentatively plan to end at the end of this month. Maybe we can work a little more on your relationship to Sam.

2. IN the first interviews and beginning stages of therapy, a middle-aged man only moderately troubled by a compulsive neurosis made good progress. However, as time went by the therapist began to feel that beneath the neurotic defenses lay a schizophrenia. The patient, for no clearly explicable reasons, became more and more upset by the interviews despite a reduction in their frequency and a change in the therapeutic technique. (cf. Chapter 9.) Hence the therapist decides that even though the patient is interested in continuing, therapy is too disruptive and should be concluded, to allow previous natural compensatory mechanisms to reinstitute an equilibrium as they had spontaneously done in the past.

THER.: If it's all right with you, I think we should interrupt our work for the time being. These spells of hysteria and crying after the interviews indicate that this treatment is too upsetting for you. At this time it's doing you more harm than good.

PT.: You feel I'm not responding the way I should?

The patient takes the suggestion as an implied accusation that he is not cooperating.

THER.: Not at all. Don't feel that I'm dissatisfied with our results so far. I think we've made some progress. Perhaps we have been going too fast and you haven't had a chance to assimilate some of the things you've learned. At any rate I suggest we discontinue for a few months. Let me see you off and on during that time and maybe later we can consider regular interviews again.

THE patient will be followed, of course, but plans for future therapy will be influenced by the principle that often it is best to leave well enough alone.

Many patients expect that something different or special will take place in the last few interviews. Some expect a summary of their problems and therapy, others anticipate that finally, as they have hoped all along, a wise authority will advise them what to do. If these expectations are evident, the therapist may interpret them, using the methods of the middle stages. Usually in the final interview the therapist makes some kind of statement that his door is open, that he will be glad to help in the future if he can.

Psychotherapists who rotate through a clinic have the problem of ending treatment when the time comes for them to leave the service. It need not be as much of a problem as it sometimes is if the patient is informed of this eventuality in the very beginning of therapy. Beginning therapists, because of their own anxieties about the patient's reactions, are often loath to do this and then find themselves and their patients in a mess when the news is suddenly broken a week or two before ending. If it is felt that the patient can profit from further work and he wishes to go on, then another therapist should take over. Neither the patient nor the therapist should believe that there is only one person in the world fit to do the job.

There are no rules about how long psychotherapy should last. Each case is unique. Cures or improvements may require a few months to several years. Patients with schizophrenias may be in treatment for many years to a lifetime. Finding briefer methods of doing the work is a problem for organized research. The beginning clinician must content himself with managing as correctly as possible the techniques thus far known to be effective.

Chapter 9

SCHIZOPHRENIAS

Everything that we have said thus far about psychotherapy is subject to modification in the schizophrenias. By "schizophrenias" (admittedly a semantic monstrosity) I mean that group of psychological conditions characterized by the patient's inability, of varying degree, to distinguish psychic thought from material reality. Material reality consists of perceptions which can be made to appear and disappear through motor activity. Everyone—normal, neurotic, and psychotic—has at times some degree of difficulty in differentiating what perceptions are realistic and what perceptions originate from mental processes. In normal and neurotic ego states the person can recognize unrealities spontaneously or when they are pointed out to him. Psychotic ego states hinder the function of this differential in proportion to their mild, moderate, or severe extent.

In Chapter 1, it was stated that neurotic symptoms result from conflicts between wish-impulses and defenses. By abolishing, modifying, or increasing the defense of wish-defense conflicts, symptoms can be removed or attenuated. The technical devices utilized in an uncovering therapy are designed to decrease the defenses of a neurotic ego which for the most part can correctly assess reality. For example, when it is demonstrated to him, the neurotic patient can understand and be convinced that his transference feelings are unrealistic, not being based on realistic knowledge of the therapist but arising from an image in his mind determined by his past.

But in the schizophrenias an already shattered ego defense structure, unable in large degree to judge reality and hence to cope with it adequately, is trying to reconstitute itself by adding and strengthening defenses. A psychotic ego attempts to heal itself by becoming neurotic. Thus psychotherapy in the schizophrenias is mainly covering, i.e., defense-adding, rather than uncovering, in order to aid spontaneous healing processes. The aim of such therapy is to convert a psychotic ego state into a normal or neurotic one and enhance its reality-testing.

The modifications of therapy to be suggested apply to schizophrenias often called "ambulatory" or "latent." They pertain to nonhospitalized patients who come voluntarily for help an hour or two a week, who thus have a sufficient residue of reality sense to realize that they are ill and who can form a friendly attachment to a therapist whose statements they deem deserving of attention. The management of each case is directly dependent on the state of this attachment and on the patient's degree of reality-testing.

Before entering a discussion of techniques, let us first consider what I feel to be the chief error made in the psychotherapy of schizophrenias. It is that the therapist does not recognize he is dealing with a schizophrenia at all. The patient is mistakenly viewed and treated as a neurotic. Such an error results from an inaccurate or incomplete concept of schizophrenic symptomatology. Textbook descriptions emphasizing delusions, hallucinations, ideas of reference, and so forth are misleading, since they portray advanced psychotic conditions and overlook the milder forms. Hence the following section on diagnosis of schizophrenias is included to acquaint the beginning therapist with common clinical pic-

tures made up of the more subtle and less conspicuous signs
and symptoms of this type of ego-state.

Diagnosis

No single sign or symptom determines a diagnosis of
schizophrenia. A neurotic patient may have one or two of
any of the following traits. It is when several of them combine to form a constellation of related symptoms that a
schizophrenic process is diagnosable.

In the beginning interviews, the psychotic patient may
appear extremely anxious, glancing about the room with a
startled or suspicious look. His eyes may dart from side to
side or the eyelids widen momentarily to reveal unusually
large areas of the white sclerae. Though looking intently at
the therapist with the first handshake (often presenting a
flaccid, cold, but sweating hand), he may from then on constantly avert his eyes from the therapist's gaze. He rigidly
holds his body in one position for a long time. Sometimes
he has a small characteristic gesture which, until one is used
to it, does not harmonize with what is being spoken. Before
an interview has ended, he may suddenly arise to leave.

The verbal behavior may have several typical qualities.
Many polysyllabic words are used in a stilted, somewhat pe-
dantic manner, as if the word itself were more important
than the facts it describes. The patient speaks in vague and
spreading generalities, so that even after he has described at
length what troubles him, one is not quite sure exactly or
specifically what does. In the description it often sounds as
if he were a distant spectator of himself or a reporter of
another person. The content of his speech is unusual.
Neurotic patients—except psychologically lettered intellec-
tuals who have decided from their reading what should be
brought out in therapy—do not immediately or easily speak

of sexual, incestuous, homicidal, or certain bodily topics. It is only after the usual resistances against expressing such ideas have been gradually removed in therapy that they are verbalized. But in schizophrenia the patient may in the first interview blandly speak of desires to have intercourse with his mother, impulses to eat another's feces, or wishes to exhibit his genitals. In other words, there are too few resistances against discussing instinctual impulses rather than too many. Thus if the patient were allowed to free-associate, it would be observed that he associates literally too freely, producing a chaotic mass of disconnected thoughts lacking in the ordinary conversational restraints of propriety. On the other hand he may show great reluctance and discomfort in telling something which when revealed seems (to the therapist, but obviously not to the patient) unwarranting of that much turmoil. For example a slim and attractive girl struggled for weeks to tell her therapist the secret though real cause of all her difficulties—namely, that she was fat.

Common symptoms complained of are fatigue, disinterest, and lack of concentration. The patient may experience diffuse and fluctuating sensations of unreality. He feels estranged from the world around him, and internally he feels as if something has fallen away, leaving him hollow inside. Such a depersonalization is often accompanied by a hypochondriacal preoccupation with body surfaces, orifices, and organs. Periods of being unable to feel strongly about anything are punctuated by outbursts of intense emotions, particularly of rage. Any of the neurotic symptoms may develop in a mild to severe form. In fact if a patient shows several symptoms typical of different neuroses, e.g., phobias, compulsions, and conversions, one should look for further evidence of a schizophrenia. Severe depressions in young people and severe hysterias at any age are significant indications worth keeping in mind.

The patient's daily thought and behavior contain certain elements of diagnostic significance. Long, involved, and dramatic day-dreams may occupy much of his attention. They are full of murders, grandiose accomplishments, widespread destruction, and sexual orgies. Sexual thoughts concern polymorphous perverse activities—exhibitionism, incest, sado-masochism. In his sexual life he prefers masturbation, engaging in it several times a day, often without any accompanying fantasies. Or he may have extremely frequent intercourse, during which he may be anesthetic and have no fantasies or the latter may be of a sado-masochistic nature. Perversions such as transvestitism, fetishism, or exhibitionism are often the living-out of a psychotic ego state.

Patients with schizophrenias become successively fascinated with all sorts of esoteric cults, fads, and mystical systems of thought. They show an eager curiosity about complex religious and philosophic questions. Psychological theories, electronic machines, and currently publicized sciences such as cybernetics or semantics are favorite subjects. As one interest fades, another takes its place. The patient may subject himself to various rituals or procedures demanded by the cult, for example, dieting, practicing eye-movements, or prolonged meditation. Although he allies himself with groups in this fashion, he seldom feels close to anyone in the group. Isolated from other isolated people, he soon begins to feel they do not like him or they are against him and he leaves, later to find another group and repeat the whole cycle again.

The past history of the patient offers further diagnostic material. One or both parents may have been psychotic. If she is not psychotic, the mother is often a highly narcissistic person who cannot "give" to her children, especially during their first year of life. The patient's childhood experiences include frequent severe anxieties, panics, or even true delusions. It may be discovered that he has always been greatly upset by environmental changes such as a new school or a new house. A history of alcoholism in adolescence or a prolonged period of bed rest at this time without evidence of a serious physical disease often indicates transient psychotic episodes. Attempts (sometimes successful) to have the nose, lips, or forehead changed by plastic surgery are frequently observed in schizophrenias. A long history of a severe "psychosomatic" disease such as eczema or colitis should induce the therapist to look for further signs and symptoms as outlined above.

Finally in the therapeutic interviews a few phenomena may herald a psychotic ego state. The sudden improvement or disappearance of a long-standing neurotic symptom after only a few hours of therapy often occurs in schizophrenias. The patient may show extreme sensitivity to the therapist's statements or facial expressions. He dreams profusely and is often extremely disturbed by the bizarre nature of the dreams. They involve scenes of mass destruction, weird animal or insect-like shapes, and bodily distortions and mutilations.

A patient showing several of the mechanisms we have described should make the therapist think of schizophrenia. To make this diagnosis is more than an academic question, because psychotherapy in a schizophrenia differs widely from psychotherapy in a neurosis. The ways in which it differs will now be discussed from the standpoint of the topics considered in the book thus far.

Time and Space Conditions

Beginning and ending the interview can be leniently arranged. A resistance of late-coming need not be discussed. If the patient strongly feels at any time during the hour that he wants to leave, he should be allowed this freedom. The therapist should not terminate the interview if the patient appears confused or uncertain about some point discussed. Often it is helpful to make a brief summary of the interview's main points at the end of each hour.

A patient enveloped in magical thinking may look on many of the objects in the therapist's office as having some hidden significance. This is particularly true in the case of a couch. Most therapists feel that patients with difficulty in reality-testing should not be placed on a couch, since it adds to the "unreal" quality of therapy.

Interview Behavior

The patient is extremely alert to everything the therapist says or does. The therapist's gestures, changes in position, and facial expressions may be perceived as having double, personal, or magical meanings for him. Slight indications of exasperation or hostility are watched for, and when discovered they are felt as major rejections. Hence in his actions and attitudes the therapist should lean toward a more friendly, benevolent, accepting, and giving role than is required in treating neuroses. One accepts gifts with thanks, carefully observes the claims of etiquette, takes the patient's side in family conflicts—all in an attempt to gain and preserve friendly transferences. H. Sullivan's deft advice is that the therapist should try to avoid collisions with the patient's self-esteem. This attitude can be carried out within the bounds of a professional relationship. Moving too close interpersonally to a patient can frighten or antagonize him just as much as remaining too distant.

Relatives can be interviewed only with the patient's permission. He should be allowed to sit in on the interview, especially if he may be suspicious that the therapist is really an ally of parents or relatives trying to force him to live according to their rules and desires. If he is not present, he should be told later what was said. No guile or lies, however white, are permissible.

In working with out-patients once or twice a week, the therapist must be prepared to deal with telephone calls between interviews. They may be of great significance in the patient's repeated testing to see if there really is a reliable person taking an interest in him.

The First Interviews

With neuroses the technique of the early interviews involves alternate silences and interpositions, usually questions. But with psychoses there is a quantitative change in that the therapist makes less use of silence. Silence becomes dreadedly loud in these patients' ears, and it is interpreted by them as a reticence due to disinterest or dislike. When the patient stops talking and appears to be struggling with the silence, one helps him to start up again with a question or some other interposition. Also in this regard, the therapist never meets a question from the patient with silence but makes some response to it. Thus, in general, the therapist is more active and directive in questioning, focusing, explaining, i.e., interposing.

Questions should be asked with a minimum spirit of quizzing or probing. Nor should they carry an air of being heavily weighted with significance. Attempts to pry into his deeper thoughts and fantasies too soon invariably lead the patient to recoil all the more from an at best tenuous relationship. As P. Federn has stated, the therapist should not try to uncover the details of previous psychotic episodes. Any areas of the patient's life for which he has an amnesia should not be tampered with. Such spontaneous resolutions of conflicts through strong repressions are defenses best left intact.

During the beginning stages of therapy and long into the middle course of the treatment, the therapist must agree with the patient's ideas, however unrealistic they are. This does not mean that a delusion is actually confirmed, but neither is it directly opposed by the therapist. This technique is illustrated in the following example:

CONVINCED that his next-door neighbors don't like him and do various things to inconvenience him, a seclusive man has fits of rage. His family tells him his ideas are all nonsense, but of course it only adds to his rage that they should ally themselves with the neighbors.

In the first interview he asks the therapist for an opinion about his ideas.

PT.: Do you think it's my imagination, that I'm crazy as they say?
THER.: From what you've told me, it's hard to tell what is going on there with your neighbors. It can't be *all* your imagination. Maybe it's a mixture of things, a little of both.
PT.: Yes, that makes sense. But I can't understand what they would have against me.

THE important point here is not that the therapist's statement intends to shake the patient's belief but that the therapist does not act like others in trying to argue him out of it. Instead he allows room for the patient's belief to have some justification. Repeated experiences of this kind with his therapist will eventually make it possible for the patient to be influenced by one who understands him and respects his views.

In contrast to the technique suitable for neuroses, the therapist does not in early interviews attempt vigorously to elucidate a major area of conflict. Rather, in learning about the patient, he tries to evaluate in which areas the patient's ego functions adequately (i.e., normally or neurotically) and in what areas the ego has difficulty in reality perception and testing. Once the latter becomes clear, therapy can be directed toward nursing a seedling of reasonable ego to extend into some of those areas. The major life area to be clarified and understood for its realistic-unrealistic components is the patient's relationship to people. His withdrawal and isolation based on fears or resentments are defenses eventually suitable for interpretive modification. All natural restitutive symptoms such as hallucinations, world-reconstruction fantasies, and encapsulated, systematized projections should be respected for their healing functions and left unprobed.

When the patient urgently expresses his fears of insanity, homicide, or suicide, they should be frankly discussed. The therapist's own apprehensive reluctance to enter these topics may serve to frighten the patient further. Such fears are not entirely baseless in schizophrenias and must be treated with a calm thoroughness which attempts to stress the wide separation between thought and act.

One type of interposition common in the beginning, as well as at other stages of the therapy, consists of advice. At times the therapist must offer practical suggestions to the patient whose reality judgment is so impaired as to jeopardize his best interests. For example, a patient whose concept of his body is distorted may be advised not to undergo the plastic surgery he has planned. Or it may be suggested that a patient change his living quarters where he is under the constant unnerving pressure of homosexual feelings toward a room-mate. As with all advice-giving on the part of the therapist, it should be done cautiously and in small doses. The therapist must be prepared for the prospect that often his advice will not be taken or, even worse, that it will be followed but have bad results.

The Middle Period

It is typical of one with a psychotic ego state that he has no difficulty in being or becoming aware of his basic instinctual wish-impulses. However, this "tragic miracle of consciousness" handicaps rather than aids him. His preoccupation with a welter of erupting impulses serves to estrange him further from a real world of people and events. Hence in interpretation the therapist in general does not confront the patient with warded-off impulses but with the way in which the patient is concerned with these impulses in order to ward off reality. The therapist in interpreting disregards the actual content of day-dreams, fantasies, and ruminations and centers his discussion around their use as a defense against reality, as in the following example:

WHEN trying to complete routine homework requiring continued concentration but no original inventiveness, a mathematics student would drift off into reverie at his desk. He describes seeing himself on a platform in the stadium before thousands of people. He and a beautiful girl perform an orgy of intercourse followed by eating and smearing one another with feces. The patient wishes to enter a discussion of the content of this fantasy.

PT.: When I thought about the day-dream it seemed to prove my anal impulses. Do you think my trouble is that I'm really an anal-erotic?
THER.: Oh, I don't know if that's so important. I'm more interested in the fact that you get this day-dream when you are working. Perhaps when the homework bores you, you try to escape it by day-dreaming.
PT.: Those problems he gives us every night are a waste of time. A child could do them. And what gets me is that so much of my grade is based on them.
THER.: That's why this is an important point. The only good reason for doing the problems is to pass the course. They probably are an insult to your intelligence, and you avoid them

out of resentment toward your professor. But if, as you say, you are really interested in a degree you will inevitably have to do things you don't like.

RATHER than become involved in the instinctual material, the therapist deals with the patient's interpersonal basis of avoidance of realities important for his long-range life goal.

The therapist's interpositions and interpretations should repeatedly emphasize the patient's present life situation and how he is meeting it. The problems of day-to-day living are gone over, often paying attention to the smallest details, e.g.:

As has been her custom, a young woman begins the hour with an exposition of her idea that all the members of her family are against her. She repeats the grievances that the therapist has heard numberless times before. Instead of allowing her to go on into the complex ramifications of her idea, the therapist by his questions focuses the patient's attention on her reality life.

THER.: Now could you tell me what you have been doing this week?
PT.: Tuesday I went shopping. I was looking for a certain kind of brooch to replace one I had lost or maybe it was stolen. I wouldn't put it past my sister to do something like that.

Drifting into her suspicions again.

THER. (interrupting): And after the shopping?
PT.: I met a friend for lunch. She's the girl I told you about last time. We had lunch at the hotel. I began to feel uncomfortable there.
THER.: What was upsetting you?
PT.: Others looking at me, I guess. Worried about my appearance.

She now goes to the topic of her social anxiety, a subject that is usually fruitful for investigation and interpretation.

Once the patient begins to trust the therapist and form a friendly attachment to him (this may take a long time), he can be influenced little by little to accept alternate realistic explanations of events which trouble him. The types of transferences developed by the patient are exactly like those described for neuroses. Contrary to former opinions, they may be just as intense, though less apparent, than transferences made by other patients. In fact those transferences ascribing a magical parental omnipotence to the therapist are often accentuated.

Aiding the patient's reality-testing means to offer views different from his, relying on the transference attachment to win his giving them serious thought. The therapist's alternate views are formed with the aid of his own reality sense, some of which he then attempts to put at the disposal of the patient, as in the following procedure:

A SENSITIVE and distrustful office worker is certain that many of the activities in his office have reference to him. The therapist has never contradicted these thoughts, letting them pass by. At this point in therapy, however, he feels that the patient might listen to another explanation without feeling so injured as to withdraw his friendliness for the therapist.

The patient has just mentioned that a colleague closed a window in the office, intending to stifle him.

THER.: What gave you the feeling he did it to inconvenience you?
PT.: Because I had opened it a few hours before, so he knew I wanted it open.
THER.: Do you think he remembered it was you who opened it?
PT.: I don't know. There are so many people in that office. Why?
THER.: I know how you feel about your fellow-workers there, but in this case of the window I was thinking there might be another explanation for it. Namely that he closed the window without thinking about you at all. I could imagine that he didn't know who opened it, that he closed it only for his own comfort, and that he had no intention of bothering anybody.

PT.: Could be. But it does bother me to have the window closed.
THER.: Sure it does. Because you feel bothered, maybe that's
why you think someone is trying to bother you. But you can
see that if something results within you, it doesn't necessarily
follow that that was its original purpose.

THE therapist tries to teach the patient to distinguish between a
purely inner experience and an outer event.

Thus in learning to test reality the patient with the help
of the therapist goes over dozens and hundreds of daily
experiences seeking to recognize the difference between what
actually occurs in the external world and what he interprets as
occurring according to distortions produced by his own inner
ideas. Out of this process an identification develops with
the therapist's normal adult ego state and the patient slowly
gains reality sense and begins to layer over remaining unrealistic concepts with more conventional attitudes, i.e., to
"make like normal."

Since many patients tend spontaneously to intellectualize,
the therapist may try to capitalize on this resistance through
offering psychological information and explanations. By
fostering the patient's intellectualized defenses, an increase
in base-line resistances is therapeutically induced to provide
reinforcement for a friable ego. For example:

So great was his anxiety around people whom he did not know
that a librarian could not enter a restaurant alone. Also if someone looked at him on the street, he felt uneasy and wanted to
get away. Knowing from other evidence that the patient felt
very guilty about his secret sexual fantasies, the therapist had one
day casually stated to him that the reason he felt anxious around
people was his unnecessary fear that they could read his sexual
thoughts. During subsequent weeks the patient lost a large
part of his social anxiety and could move freely among strange
people.
How the interpretation, perhaps relevant but somewhat too
glib and inexact, was put to use by the patient is shown in this

interview months later. In passing the patient mentions his old anxiety.

THER.: Looking back, what do you think it was you were afraid of around people?

PT. (*immediately unsettled*): But didn't you say it was because I feared they could tell about my sexual thoughts?

THER.: That's right.

PT. (*relieved*): Well, then I said to myself, "How could they know what I thought?" And knowing they can't, there's nothing to be afraid of.

THE therapist sees that his previous interpretation was accepted by the patient as the reason for his anxiety. Ascribing his anxiety to the explanation given by an authority who "knows things," he is able to reassure himself there is no need to be afraid because he has sufficient reality-sense to know that people cannot tell what he is thinking.

Not all of the therapeutic work is intended to help a psychotic ego to mend fences through adding defenses. Certain symptoms can be treated by attempts to lessen the defenses involved. Social anxiety based on a projected fear of punishment, withdrawal, and some types of guilt feeling are common problems in which the superego burden may be ameliorated. Also each patient may have some particular conflict which the therapist judges can best be handled by an uncovering interpretation rather than by a covering inter-position, as in this example:

THE thirty-year-old virgin daughter of a clergyman enjoyed smok-ing the few times she tried it. However, after each intemperance she felt she had sinned and became depressed. During therapy the patient had begun to smoke an occasional cigarette, partially out of identification with the therapist. In this hour she de-scribes her guilt and its relation to violating her father's command, then asks:

Pt.: What do you think about my smoking?

Ther.: I don't think smoking is such a sin. Part of you thinks so because your father says so, but I feel your father is overly stern in this respect. Smoking is a small pleasure that you should feel free to enjoy.

The patient seeks permission for an instinctual pleasure from a substitute father. He gives it hoping to diminish a reaction formation and allow fuller impulse gratification.

It cannot be overstressed that a friendly transference is the fulcrum for effective psychotherapy with these patients. Once the patient becomes persistently antagonistic or involves the therapist in persecutory delusions, therapy should be discontinued without attempting to work it out. Often a trial with another therapist, allowing the first to be the needed recipient of displaced hatred, will prove more successful. Transference resistances, which may supplement defenses against a psychotic engulfment, should be permitted to function for a long time, perhaps forever, without interpretation.

A few conflicts may be worked through in the way described for neuroses in the preceding chapter. But the bulk of therapeutic work consists of repeated efforts to help the patient discriminate between his wishes and fears and external reality. Concentrating on his manner of relating to people rather than his interest in words and abstract ideas, therapy can convert the patient's psychotic level of adaptation to a normal-neurotic one with relief of his distressing symptoms.

Ending Therapy

The same principles for ending apply here as were outlined for neuroses. If at any time the patient wishes to interrupt therapy, he should be allowed to do so, even in the face of objections from relatives or friends. Those patients who wish to continue, though further therapeutic work seems hopeless, should not be completely denied the opportunity to talk over their problems with a therapist. They can be seen at infrequent intervals and, as happens in a clinic, by a succession of therapists. Often through interviews held only once a month or even once or twice a year, a patient can function within the equilibrium of a compensated neurotic-psychotic ego state for life.

An Illustrative Series of Interviews

To illustrate some of the technical modifications discussed, several interviews from the middle of therapy in a clinical case are presented.

THE patient is an intelligent young woman in her early twenties. She comes to therapy complaining of anxiety attacks, depression, and confusion about her position in life. At present she stays at home with her parents, going out only to shop. Until a year ago she attended college, but she found the work too hard. She describes her father as a friendly, jovial man with whom she is on good terms. Her mother appears as an aloof, cold queen—always poised and unbending. In an interview with the therapist, the mother disclosed her conviction that the patient is mentally deficient and hence needs firm guidance. The therapist's doubting of her opinion about her daughter's intelligence only confirmed her view that he was a fool who must be tolerated for the time being, since the patient insists on consulting him.

The only child born into this family of a middle socio-economic level, the patient grew up in a sheltered and restricted atmosphere. Due to the mother's concern over intelligence as an asset, emphasis was placed in childhood training on precocious mental development. The patient was taught to read and count at a very early age, but on entering school at five she showed only average ability. However, the mother continued to push her toward intellectual pursuits. The patient replied with a subtle but forceful resistance which the mother came to interpret as intellectual deficiency. Throughout high school she had few friends and no dates. Entering college, she suddenly became aware that something was amiss psychologically when she compared herself with her contemporaries. Her first outspoken defiance of her mother was to seek psychotherapy.

Further symptoms suffered by the patient are a feeling of being alone in the world, severe fears of night monsters, sensations of unreality, and ideas that people look at her queerly. Since she was nine when she developed a sudden panic at the thought that she was alone in the world, she has fluctuated between thinking that other people exist and feeling that they are only products of her mind. Adolescence found her secretly investigating various religious and philosophic creeds in an effort to solve the problem. Unknown to her parents, she became a Catholic for a few years, but this also failed to quiet her wonder. The night monsters she fears originated in childhood and persist in a less intense manner up to the present time. She has difficulty going to bed and falling asleep because she begins to think the room is swarming with large, hairy spiders or that some type of octopus with teeth is creeping up on her. Ideas that people are looking at her and that her surroundings are unreal occur only when she is on the street.

In character structure the patient makes liberal use of compulsive mechanisms. She is orderly and perfectionistic about her room and clothes. But outside of concern for what she wears, she lacks interest in other activities, preferring to ruminate about the meanings of life and death, the real and the unreal, being and not being. She is reserved and shy, keeps her thoughts to herself, lets her mother make all decisions for her, and has little to say when spoken to, thus giving to others an impression of mental retardation. Her appearance and actions are those of an adolescent girl rather than of a woman her age.

The patient has a psychotic ego state in which her level of functioning represents mainly an arrest rather than a fixation. Psychotherapy can hope to help her grow further, diminish her withdrawal, and aid her reality-testing. The interviews now reported occurred over a period of months of therapy. The therapist's technique during this time involved concentrating on her feelings about people, especially her parents, and avoiding discussions of her philosophic preoccupations. Only once did she say anything about the therapist. Toward him she behaved girlishly, with a mixture of obvious admiration and a pinch of flirtatiousness.

Interview 10.

TODAY the patient begins by pondering out loud over the principles of an occult sect she has studied which believes the meaning of life lies in a correct appreciation of nature, especially trees. After some minutes of this, the therapist interrupts to bring the patient back to her daily reality life.

THER.: Now tell me what you have been doing since last week.
PT.: Nothing, really. I cleaned up my room, read a lot, tried some sewing. Day-dreamed most of the time. This idea about trees I gave a lot of thought to. There might be something in it.

SHE returns to her intellectual defenses against reality. Rather than get involved in the content of the tree philosophy, the therapist talks of the use the patient makes of it.

THER.: Do you ever feel you are more interested in thinking about, rather than in living, your life?
PT.: I don't have anything else to do but think. It passes the time. What else can I do?

Asking for advice which the therapist in this situation gladly gives.

THER.: I feel it would help you to take up some regular activity, get interested in doing something. For instance, you mentioned once you would like to learn how to drive a car. Have you considered that again?
PT.: I have. I'm not sure mother would approve. She's afraid I'm so nervous that I would have an accident. Could I have her call you about it?
THER.: Why don't you discuss it with her if you're really interested? If there's any doubt in her mind, ask her to phone me.

ENCOURAGING the patient to attempt mastery of a reality area, the therapist offers his support in dealing with her mother's possible objections. By offering advice of this kind he seeks to direct at least a small portion of her mental activity outward, away from inner abstract preoccupations.

THER.: What sort of terms are you on with your mother these days?

AGAIN influencing her to talk about interpersonal problems. The remainder of the hour she talked of her mixed love and resentment toward her mother. In general the interview is maintained on a supportive and conversational level. The next interview illustrates a bit of uncovering work.

Interview 26.

THE hour opens with the patient's typical backwardness in starting to talk. The therapist shows his interest by immediately asking a question rather than letting her carry the burden of silence.

THER.: What are you interested in talking about today?
PT.: My loneliness, I guess. I feel I don't have anyone really close to me. I don't even want to see my old friends any more. They weren't really friends, just acquaintances I hung around with. They didn't do me any good, and I didn't like the way they lived. . . .

These were a promiscuous group of artists she had known for a short time in college.

PT.: . . . The other day I met a girl I knew in high school and she invited me to her house, but I refused. She bores me. There's nothing we can talk about.
THER.: Do you feel your loneliness is the outcome of your own activity?
PT.: In a way. What do you mean by my activity?
THER.: I mean that maybe you are lonely because you have removed yourself from people. Like with this girl.
PT.: But that's only true in a few cases. A few people I don't like and avoid. The rest is because of my fear. I'm afraid to meet new people, strangers. Mother tries to get me to join clubs and go to parties, but I always make some excuse.

THER.: What is it you fear from strangers?

PT.: Talking to them. I can't think of anything to say. Then I know they'll think I'm a dope. When I meet someone I freeze. They're sizing me up. Sooner or later they will ask me what I am doing and I'll have to say "nothing." What should they think of someone who doesn't work, doesn't go to school, doesn't do anything but sit at home?

THER.: So you fear they will look down on you.

Approaches the patient's projection of superego values onto others.

PT.: They must. They think I'm worthless, inferior.

THER.: Can you give me a specific example of meeting someone and feeling this way?

THUS far the discussion has concerned a general "they." By asking for details about a specific experience, the therapist focuses her attention on her feelings as arising from interpersonal relationships. She tells of trying to converse with a woman her age but failing because the woman was a college graduate and must have regarded as inferior those who were not. The patient then talked of her guilt about quitting school, since it meant she was a misfit. The therapist interprets her fear of people's opinion as fear of her own.

THER.: It's interesting that the low opinions you fear others will have of you are exactly the opinions part of you has about yourself.

PT.: You mean I assume others think the way I do?

THER.: Yes. You ascribe to this college woman a view that is really your own. You regard yourself as a misfit for not finishing college and then project that evaluation onto people you meet.

THE patient is shown one of her psychological mechanisms in the same manner as would be attempted in a neurosis. No impulses are touched upon. Only defenses against projected superego anxiety are mentioned. This type of uncovering is permissible and valuable in such a case.

Interview 43.

AT this point in therapy there have been a few changes in the patient's life. Freed of some of her social inhibitions, she has developed a friendship with a girl who is also learning to drive a car. The confidence gained through mastering an auto and increasing the range of her mobility in the external world have added to her hope that she can be like others. In the therapist she has found an ally she can depend on during her ambivalent anxiety in moving out from under her mother's thumb.

She mentions a dream of the previous night.

PT.: Had a weird dream last night. I was in a bedroom somewhere. On the bed there was an older woman, naked, with some pearls around her neck. She put her arms out to me as if asking me to come nearer. Then another girl ran into the room with a hatchet or a cleaver and started hacking up the woman. I awoke with a start. What a horrible dream! Then all of a sudden I thought there was something in the room. I put the light on but nothing was there. What do you think the dream means? The older woman could be my mother. I have felt like killing her at times.

Too true to be good for this patient. The murderous, mutilative, and homosexual impulses in the dream should not be uncovered. The dream can be discussed briefly, using a technique of allaying anxiety by "naming it."

THER.: When you woke up you were frightened by something that might be in the room to hurt you?
PT.: Yes. Much like the fear I have when falling asleep.
THER.: As you say, the dream might be an expression of normal death wishes that we all have toward our parents at some time or other. And the fear of something hurting you would be the fear of punishment for those death wishes. Maybe those things you fear when you go to sleep represent severe punishments for what you feel are sins.

Explaining, psychologizing, and implanting intellectual defenses.

PT.: They began when I was small, and I certainly had a great fear of punishment then. Not physical punishment, but being scolded and criticized. My mother could make me feel guilty just with a glance, even when I hadn't done anything.

She continues in the direction of describing some of her life as a child and the various means she evolved to deceive or oppose her mother.

Interview 65.

This interview is selected because this is the only time that the patient's feelings toward the therapist were mentioned. Thus far in therapy the situations which in neuroses would require transference interpretations, i.e., intercurrent resistances, have been managed by interpositions alone. But in this hour the patient seems unable to overcome a reluctance to speak, even though helped by questions from the therapist. Applying the principle of bringing up the transference when confronted by a strong resistance, the therapist begins.

Ther.: You seem a little reluctant to talk today.
Pt.: I suppose so.
Ther.: What do you think the reason is?
Pt.: Can't think of much to say. I'm all talked out.
Ther.: Maybe it has something to do with me.
Pt.: What do you mean?
Ther.: That you are reluctant to talk because you have something on your mind regarding me.
Pt.: No. I don't think so.

No success, so the therapist tries a different angle of approach.

Ther.: Even if it isn't on your mind now, what have been your thoughts about me?
Pt.: Oh, I've had all kinds. At first I didn't trust you. Especially when I thought you would tell everything I told you to my mother. That's what another doctor did once. After you saw my mother, I quizzed her about it and compared what she said to what you said was talked about. It was close enough so that I trusted you a little more. But even nowadays sometimes I wonder how much I should tell you.

THER.: Is it only that you're afraid I'll tell your mother what we talk about?

PT.: Not entirely. I worry how you will react. Whether you will ridicule me or look disgusted with me.

THER.: Whether I'll react like your mother?

PT.: I suppose so. Another thing I feared was that you had dictaphones in here or a camera taking a picture.

THER.: What made you think of those things?

PT.: Sometimes I hear a whirring noise as if a machine was running.

THER.: Oh, that's just the ventilating system going on and off. There are no cameras or dictaphones in here.

HE explains the reality factor and ignores pointing out the mildly paranoid aspects of her thinking. Returning to her distrust:

THER.: And today is it that you are wondering if you can trust telling me something?

PT.: This isn't trust so much as a fear of your reaction. So you must know what it is.

THER.: No, I don't.

PT. (*with great hesitation*): Well—it's sex. To be more specific, masturbation.

HER first mention in six months of a sexual topic. The patient continues to talk of her anxieties about infrequent masturbation. The transference in this instance is hardly explored beyond the connection between therapist and mother. However, with the resistance removed for the time being, further transference discussion is not required.

A therapist, sharing our culture's rush for change, may become disheartened in treating schizophrenia when immediate improvements are not forthcoming. But many psychotic ego states are reversible, requiring only patient psychotherapeutic work over a long period of time. In fact some of the best results effected by psychotherapy can be achieved in these cases.

INDEX OF SUBJECTS

INDEX OF NAMES